ONE

NONE

AND

A HUNDRED-THOUSAND

A Novel

BY

LUIGI PIRANDELLO

Author of "Tonight We Improvise," "As You Desire Me,"
"Six Characters in Search of an Author," etc.

Translated from the Italian
BY SAMUEL PUTNAM

NEW YORK

E. P. DUTTON & CO., INC.

NOTE

"This book not only depicts dramatically, but at the same time demonstrates by what might be termed a mathematic method, the impossibility of any human creature's being to others what he is to himself.

"If you would like to have an idea of how it is that others see you, so as no longer to have to marvel at the judgments which others pass upon your personality, learn to reflect like the hero of this novel."

LUIGI PIRANDELLO.

CONTENTS

BOOK FIRST

BOOK SECOND

CONTENTS—Continued

CONTENTS—Continued

CONTENTS—Continued

BOOK FIRST

BOOK FIRST.

I

My Wife and My Nose

"WHAT are you doing?" my wife asked me, as she saw me lingering, contrary to my wont, in front of the mirror.

"Nothing," I told her. "I am just having a look here, in my nose, in this nostril. It hurts me a little, when I take hold of it."

My wife smiled.

"I thought," she said, "that you were looking to see which side it is hangs down the lower."

I whirled like a dog whose tail has been stepped on:

"Which side hangs down the lower? My nose? Mine?"

"Why, yes, dear," and my wife was serene, "take a good look; the right side is a little lower than the other."

I was twenty-eight years old; and up to now, I had always looked upon my nose as being, if not altogether handsome, at least a very respectable sort of nose, as might have been said of all the other parts of my person. So far as that was concerned, I had been ready to admit and maintain a point that is customarily admitted and maintained by all those who have not had the misfortune to bring a deformed body into the world, namely, that it is silly

13

to indulge in any vanity over one's personal linea-
ments.   And yet, the unforeseen, unexpected discovery of this particular defect angered me like an
undeserved punishment.   It may be that my wife
saw through this anger of mine; for she quickly
added that, if I was under the firm and comforting
impression of being wholly without blemishes, it
was one of which I might rid myself; since, just as
my nose sagged to the right—

"Something else?"

Yes, there was something else! Something else!
My eyebrows were like a pair of circumflex accents,
∧ ∧ ; my ears were badly put on, one of them standing out more than the other; and there were further
shortcomings—

"What, more?"

Ah, yes, more: my hands, the little finger; and
my legs (no! surely they were not crooked!)—the
right one was bowed slightly more than the other,
toward the knee—ever so slightly.

Following an attentive examination, I had to
admit that all these defects existed.   It was only
then, when the feeling of astonishment that succeeded my anger had definitely changed to one of
grief and humiliation—it was only then that my
wife strove to console me, urging me not to take
it so to heart, since with all my faults, when all was
said, I was still a handsome fellow.   I made the best
of it, accepting as a generous concession what had
been denied me as a right.   I let out a most venom-
ous "thanks," and, safe in the assurance that I had
no cause for either grief or humiliation, proceeded

to attribute not the slightest importance to these trifling defects; but I did confer a very great and extraordinary importance upon the fact that I had gone on living all these years without ever once having changed noses, keeping the same one all the time, and with the same eyebrows and the same ears, the same hands and the same legs—and to think that I had had to take a wife, to realize that they were not all that they should be.

"Huh! small wonder in that! Doesn't everybody know what wives are for? Made, precisely, for discovering a husband's faults."

True enough, mind you—I don't deny this about wives. But I may tell you that, in those days, I was prone to fall, at any word said to me, at the sight of a housefly[1] buzzing about, into deeps of reflection and pondering that left me with a hollow feeling inside, and which rent my soul from top to bottom and tore it inside out like a molehill, without any of all this being visible on the outside.

"It is plain to be seen," you will tell me, "that you had plenty of time to squander."

Not exactly that, I would have you know. Some allowance is to be made for the state of mind I was in. But beyond that, I don't deny that my life was leisurely to the point of idleness. I was well-to-do, and a pair of faithful friends, Sebastiano Quantorzo and Stefano Firbo, had looked after my interests since my father's death. My father, by fair means or other, had not succeeded in doing anything with

---

[1] In Italian, *mosca;* cf. the protagonist's name, *Moscarda.* (Translator.)

me, beyond seeing that I married at a very early age, possibly with the hope that I would at least provide a son who would be not at all like me; but the poor man had not been able to get even this out of me. It was not, understand, that I opposed any will of my own to taking the path upon which my father wished to embark me. I took them all. But taking them was all I did; I did not do any walking to speak of, but would come to a halt at every step, at every smallest stone I encountered, to hover about it, first at a distance and then closer up; and I wondered no little how others could go on past me, without taking any account whatever of that stone, which for me meanwhile had come to assume the proportions of an insurmountable mountain, as well as those of a world in which, without any further ado, I might have made myself at home.

I had remained halting like this at the first steps I had taken along so many paths, my mind full of worlds, or of little rocks, which amounts to the same thing. As a matter of fact, it did not seem to me that those who had passed me, and who had gone all the way, were substantially any the wiser than I. They had passed me, there was no doubt about that, prancing like colts; but at the end of the road, what they had found was a cart, their own cart; they had harnessed themselves to it with a vast deal of patience, and were now engaged in drawing it after them. But I drew no cart, and bore, accordingly, neither bridle nor blinders; I could certainly see farther than they; but go—where was there to go?

Coming back now to the discovery of those slight

defects, I was immersed all of a sudden in the reflection that it meant—could it be possible?—that I
did not so much as know my own body, the things
which were most intimately a part of me: nose, ears,
hands, legs. And turning to look at myself once
more, I examined them again. It was from there
that my sickness started, that sickness which would
speedily have rendered me so wretched and despairing of body and of mind that I should certainly have
died of it or gone mad, had I not found in my malady
itself the remedy (I may say) which was to cure
me of it.

II

And What About Your Own?

I AT once imagined that everybody, now that my wife
had made the discovery, must be aware of those
same bodily defects, and that they must see nothing
else in me.

"Is it my nose you are staring at?" I suddenly
asked a friend, that very day, who had stopped to
speak to me of some matter or other that meant a
great deal to him.

"No," he said. "Why?"

I smiled nervously:

"The right side is a little lower, haven't you
noticed?"

And I insisted upon his pausing to observe it at-
tentively, as if that defect in my nose were an
irreparable hitch that had occurred in the mechan-
ism of the universe. My friend surveyed me at first
in some astonishment; he surely suspected that my
reason for thus, suddenly and without rhyme or
reason, dragging in that remark about my nose, was
that I did not deem the business of which he had
been speaking to me worth my attention or a reply,
for he gave a shrug of the shoulders and started to
leave me, unceremoniously. I caught him by the
arm.

"No, no," I said, I am very much interested in
your proposition. But you will have to excuse me
for the moment."

"Is it your nose you're thinking of?"

"I never noticed before that it sagged to the right. My wife called my attention to it this morning."

"Really?" said my friend. His tone was questioning, and there was an incredulous and even derisive smile in his eyes.

I stood there gazing at him, as I had gazed at my wife that morning, with a mixture, that is to say, of humiliation, of anger and of astonishment. So he, too, had noticed it, had he? And how many others! How many? Yet I had been unaware of it, and, being unaware, had gone on believing that I was to everybody a Moscarda with a straight nose, whereas the truth was, every one saw me as a Moscarda with a crooked nose. And how many times, quite unsuspectingly, had I chanced to speak of Tizio or Cajo's defective nose, and how many times must I have caused a laugh, as those who heard me thought: "But just give a look at that poor chap, will you, talking about other people's faulty noses!"

It is true, I might have consoled myself with the reflection that, in the long run, my case was obviously common enough, all of which only goes to prove once again a well-known fact, namely, that we are ready enough to note the faults of others, while all the time unconscious of our own. The first germs of the malady had, however, begun to take root in my mind; and this reflection was unable to bring me any consolation. The thought, rather, remained firmly planted, that I was not for others what up to then I had inwardly pictured myself as being.

For the moment, I was thinking only of my body; and as my friend still stood there in front of me, with that derisive and incredulous air, I asked him, by way of retaliation, if he, for his part, knew that he had a dimple in his chin, which divided it into two not wholly equal parts, one of which stood out more than the other.

"I? What are you talking about! I have a dimple, I know, but it's not like what you say."

"Let's go into that barber shop over there," I suggested to him on the spur of the moment, "and you will see."

When my friend, having gone into the barber's, had satisfied himself to his own astonishment that what I had told him was true, he did his best not to display any annoyance, but observed that, when all was said, it was a trifling matter.

No doubt, he was right: it was a trifling matter; but following him at a distance, I saw him stop first at one shop window and then at another, further down the street; and then, yet further down, he came to a stop for a third time, before a shop-front mirror, to have a look at his chin; and I am quite sure that, the moment he reached his house, he must have run to the clothespress in order more conveniently to become acquainted with his new and blemished self. Nor have I the slightest doubt that, by way of avenging himself in his turn, or by way of carrying out a jest which he thought deserved to be passed along, he proceeded to treat some other friend as I had treated him, and that, after having inquired if the friend had noticed that blemish in his chin, he had gone on to discover some defect or other in his friend's forehead or mouth; while his friend, in turn —Ah, yes! ah, yes!—I could swear that, for days in a row, in the worthy city of Richieri, I saw (unless it was nothing more than my own imagination) a very considerable number of my fellow-citizens going from one shop window to another and coming to a stop before each to observe their own reflections, one to study a zygoma, another the corner of his eye, a third to examine the lobe of an ear, and a fourth to investigate his nostril. At the end of a week, moreover, a certain acquaintance accosted me; he appeared to be perplexed, and asked me if it was true that, every time he went to speak, he inadvertently contracted his left eyebrow.

"Yes, old man," I hastened to assure him. "Look at me, will you? My nose sags to the right; but I know it without your telling me. And my circumflex eyebrows! And my ears—look here—one of them stands out more than the other. And my hands—dumpy, aren't they? And the crooked joint on this little finger. And my legs—here, look at this one, this one here—does it look to you the same as the other one? It doesn't, does it? But I know it without your telling me. See you later."

I left him standing there and was on my way. I had taken but a few steps, when I heard a call:

"Ps-t!"

With the utmost serenity, the fellow buttonholed me and drew me to him.

"Excuse me," he inquired, "but your mother did not bear any other sons after you, did she?"

"No," I replied, "neither before nor after. I am an only son. Why?"

"Because," he said, "if your mother had given birth another time, it would surely have been a male."

"Yes? How do you know?"

"Listen, and I will tell you. The women of the people have a saying that, when the hair on the back of the neck ends in a little bobtail like the one you have, the next born will be a boy."

I put a hand to the back of my neck.

"Ah," I said, coldly and with the beginning of a sneer, "so I have a—what do you call it?—"

"A bobtail, old man; that's what we call it in Richieri."

"Oh, that's nothing!" I exclaimed. "I can have it cut off."

He contradicted me with his finger:

"It's a sign that will stay with you, old boy, even if you have it shaved off."

And this time, it was he who left me in the lurch.

III

A Fine Way of Being Alone!

FROM that day on, I longed most ardently to be alone, if only for an hour. It was really more than a longing; it was a need, a sharp and pressing, a restless need, which was aggravated to the point of fury by the presence or proximity of my wife.

"Did you hear what Michelina said yesterday, Gengè?[1] Quantorzo has something urgent to talk to you about."

"Look and see, Gengè, if my legs show with my dress this way."

"Gengè, the clock has stopped."

"Aren't you taking the dog out any more, Gengè? She'll ruin the carpets, then, and you'll scold her. You really ought to, you know, poor little beast— I mean—I'm not saying that— She hasn't been out since yesterday."

"Aren't you afraid, Gengè, that Anna Rosa may be ill? We haven't seen anything of her for three days now, and the last time she was here, she had a sore throat."

"Signor Firbo was here, Gengè. He said he would be back later. Couldn't you arrange to see him somewhere else? Good Lord, what a bore!"

Or else, I heard her singing:

---

[1] My wife had coined this diminutive out of Vitangelo. which is my real name, and was in the habit of calling me by it; not without reason, as will be seen further on.

E se mi dici di no,
caro il mio bene, doman non verrò;
doman non verrò . . .
doman non verrò . . .[1]

But why didn't you shut yourself in your room and blindfold your eyes if necessary?

My friends, that shows you do not understand the way in which I wanted to be alone.

The only place where I could shut myself in was my study; and even here, I did not dare put the bolt on the door, from fear of arousing unpleasant suspicions in my wife, who was, I shall not say an unpleasant woman, but a highly suspicious one. And supposing that, opening the door suddenly, she had discovered me?

No, it would not do. And anyway, it would have been useless. There were no mirrors in my study. I had need of a mirror. Furthermore, the mere thought of my wife's being in the house was sufficient to keep me in the presence of myself, which was exactly what I did not want.

What does being alone mean to you?

Keeping your own company, without any stranger about.

Ah, well, I can assure you, it's a fine way, that, of being alone. A charming little window opens for you in memory, at which, smilingly, between a vase of pinks and one of jasmine, you catch sight of Titti, knitting away at a red woolen muffler, good Lord, like the one which that impossible old Signor Giacomino wears about his neck, for whom you have

---

[1] "And if you say me no, my darling one, I will not come tomorrow," etc. (Translator.)

not yet written that letter of introduction to the president of the Association of Charities, your good friend but another terrible bore, especially when he starts talking about the fraudulent conduct of his private secretary, the one who yesterday—no, when was it?—the day before yesterday, the day it rained and the public square looked like a lake with all the raindrops glistening in a merry sprinkling of sunlight, and in the *corsa,* Lord, what a medley, the basin, the newspaper-kiosk, the tramcar threading its way through the junction and making so horrible a noise at the turn, that dog running away; but enough of this; you made your way into a billiard parlor where the secretary to the president of the Association of Charities was; and what repressed laughter there was under the big bristling mustaches, over your discomfiture, when you started playing with friend Carlino, or *Quintadecima.* And then? What happened then, when you came out of the billiard parlor? Under a languishing lamp, in the moist and deserted street, a poor melancholy drunkard was endeavoring to sing an old Neapolitan ditty, one which, all these years ago, you used to hear almost every night, in that mountain village among the chestnuts, where you had gone for an outing in order to be near that darling Mimi of yours, who afterwards married the old Commendator Della Venera and died a year later. Dear, dear Mimi! There she is, see her? at another tiny window opening for you in memory—

Yes, yes, good people, I assure you, that is a fine way of being alone, that is!

IV

The Way in Which I Wanted to Be Alone

I WANTED to be alone in an altogether unusual way, a new way. Quite the contrary of what you think: that is to say, *without myself* and, to be precise, with a stranger at hand.

Does this impress you as being a first sign of madness?

May not this be due to a lack of reflection on your part?

It may be that madness was in me already, I am not saying that it was not; but I beg you to believe that the only way of being truly alone is the one of which I am telling you.

Solitude is never where you are; it is always where you are not, and is only possible with a stranger present; whatever the place or whoever the person, it must be one that is wholly ignorant concerning you, and concerning which or whom you are equally ignorant, so that will and sensation remain suspended and confused in an anxious uncertainty, while with the ceasing of all affirmation on your part, your own inner consciousness ceases at the same time. True solitude is to be found in a place that lives a life of its own, but which for you holds no familiar footprint, speaks in no known voice, and where accordingly the stranger is yourself.

This was the way in which I wanted to be alone. Without myself. I mean to say, without that self which I already knew, or which I thought I knew. Alone with a certain stranger, from whom I darkly felt that I should be able never more to part, and who was myself: *the stranger inseparable from me.* There was, then, one only that interested me! And already, this one, or the need I felt of being alone with him, of confronting him in order to know him better and hold a little converse with him, was working me up to a pitch of half-shivering alarm.

If I was not for others what up to then I had believed myself to be to myself, what was I?

In the course of living, I had never thought of my nose, of its size, whether big or small, of the color of my eyes, or the narrowness or breadth of my forehead, and so forth. This was my nose, those were my eyes, this was my forehead; things inseparable from me, of which, immersed in my own affairs, taken up with my own ideas, given over to my own feelings, I had had no time to think.

But I was thinking now:

"And others? Others are not in me at all. For others, who look from without, my ideas, my feelings have a nose. My nose. And they have a pair of eyes, my eyes, which I do not see but which they see. What relation is there between my ideas and my nose? For me, none whatever. I do not think with my nose, nor am I conscious of my nose when I think. But others? Others, who cannot see my ideas within me, but who see my nose without? For others, there is so intimate a relation between my ideas and my nose that if the former, let us say, were very serious while the latter was mirth-provoking by reason of its shape, they would burst out laughing."

As I ran on like this, a fresh anxiety laid hold of me: the realization that I should not be able, while living, to depict myself to myself in the actions of my life, to see myself as others saw me, to set my body off in front of me and see it living like the body of another. When I took up my position in front of a mirror, something like a lull occurred inside me; all spontaneity vanished; every gesture impressed me as being fictitious or a repetition.

I could not see myself live.

I was to have a proof of this in the impression with which I was, so to speak, assailed a few days afterward, when, walking and talking with my friend, Stefano Firbo, I happened to catch an unexpected glimpse of myself in a mirror along the street, one that I had not noticed at first. This impression had not lasted more than a second, when that lull promptly occurred, spontaneity disappeared, and self-consciousness set in. I did not recognize myself at first. The impression was that of a stranger going down the street and engaged in conversation. I came to a halt. I must have been very pale.

"What's the matter?" Firbo asked me.

"It's nothing," I said. And to myself, seized by a strange fear that was at the same time a chill, I thought:

"Was it really my own, that image glimpsed in

a flash? Am I really like that, from the outside, when—all the while living—I do not think of myself? For others, then, I am that stranger whom I surprised in a mirror; I am he and not the I whom I know; I am that one there whom I myself at first, upon becoming aware of him, did not recognize. I am that stranger whom I am unable to see living except like that, in a thoughtless second. A stranger whom others alone can see and know, not I."

From that time on, I had one despairing obsession: to go in pursuit of that stranger who was in me and who kept fleeing me; whom I could not halt in front of a mirror, without his at once becoming the me that I knew; the one who lived for others and whom I could not know; whom others beheld living and not I. I wanted to see and know him, too, as others saw and knew him.

I still believed, I may repeat here, that the stranger in question was a single individual: one to all, even as I believed that I was a single individual to myself. But my atrocious drama speedily grew more complicated, with the discovery of the hundred-thousand Moscardas that I was, not only to others, but even to myself, all with the single name of Moscarda, a name that was ugly to the point of cruelty, all of them lodged within this poor body which was likewise one, one and none, alas, if I took up my position in front of a mirror and, standing motionless, looked it straight in the eyes, thereby abolishing in it all feeling and all will of its own.

It was as my drama grew thus more complicated that those fits of incredible madness came upon me.

V

In Pursuit of the Stranger

I SHALL speak now of those little games in the form of pantomime in which, in the sprightly infancy of my folly, I began to indulge in front of all the mirrors in the house, being careful to look to right and left to make sure that I was not observed by my wife, waiting eagerly until she went out to make a call or for some purchase or other, leaving me alone at last for some little time.

The thing that I strove to do was not, like a comedian, to study my movements, to compose my face for the expression of various emotions and mental impulses; on the contrary, what I wanted to do was to take myself by surprise, in my own natural actions, in those sudden alterations of countenance which accompany the mind's every movement; by way of capturing, for example, an expression of unforeseen astonishment (over every trifle, I would fling up my eyebrows to the roots of my hair and would open my eyes and mouth as widely as I could, stretching out my face as if it had been drawn by an internal wire); or a profound sorrow (and I would screw up my forehead, as I pictured the death of my wife, half-closing my eyelids, sombrely, as if brooding over my grief); or a fierce rage (and I would gnash my teeth, imagining that someone had slapped my face, and would curl up my nose, stick out my lower jaw, and flash a lightning-look).

But, first of all, that astonishment, that sorrow, that rage were feigned; they could not have been real, for the reason that had they been so, I should not have been able to view them; they would at once have ceased, owing to the very fact that I was viewing them. In the second place, the fits of astonishment that might take possession of me were exceedingly diverse in character, and the accompanying expressions were similarly and endlessly variable according to the moment and the state of mind that I was in; and the same went for all my griefs and rages. And lastly, even granting that for one single and definite feeling of astonishment, for one single and definite grief, one single and definite fit of rage, I might really have been able to assume the appropriate expressions, those expressions would have been as I saw them and not as others would have seen them. My expression of rage, for instance, would not have been the same to one who feared it, to another disposed to excuse it, to a third inclined to smile at it, and so on.

Ah! what good sense I still had, to be able to grasp all this; and yet, I was unable to make use of it, by way of drawing from the obvious impracticality of my crazy purpose the natural deduction that the best thing to do would be to renounce the hopeless undertaking and be content with living for myself, without seeing myself, and without concerning myself with any thought of others. The idea that others saw in me one that was not the I whom I knew, one whom they alone could know, as they looked at me from without, with eyes that were not my own, eyes that conferred upon me an aspect destined to remain always foreign to me, although it was one that was in me, one that was my own to them (a "mine," that is to say, that was not for me!)—a life into which, although it was my own, I had no power to penetrate—this idea gave me no rest.   How could I endure this stranger within me? This stranger who was I myself to me?   How go on not seeing him?   Not knowing him?   How remain condemned forever to bear him about with me, in me, in the sight of all others, and all the while outside my own?

VI

At Last!

"Do you know what, Gengè? Four days more have gone by. There cannot be any doubt about it, Anna Rosa must be ill. I'm going to see her."

"Dida, dear, what are you thinking of? What an idea! In this weather? Send Diego; send Nina to find out how she is. Do you want to run the risk of falling ill yourself? I won't have it, I absolutely won't have it."

When you absolutely will not have a thing, what does your wife do?

My wife, Dida, put on her bonnet. Then she handed me her cloak to hold for her. I could have leaped for joy. But Dida, in the mirror, caught sight of my smile:

"You're laughing, are you?"

"My dear, when I see how I am obeyed—"

And then, I begged her at least not to stay too long with her friend, if the latter really was suffering from a sore throat:

"A quarter of an hour, no more. Please."

In this manner, I made sure that she would not be home until nightfall. No sooner had she gone out than I spun about on my heel for joy, clapping my hands together.

"At last!"

VII

Draught of Air

I WANTED first to compose myself, to wait until every
trace of anxiety or of joy had disappeared from my
countenance, until every impulse to thought or feeling had come to a halt inside me, in order that I
might be able to take in front of the mirror a body
that was, so to speak, strange to me, and as such,
stand it up in front of me.

"Come," I said, "let's be on our way!"

I went with eyes shut and with my hands groping
before me. When I had touched the side of the
clothespress, I paused again to await, with eyes shut
still, an inner calm and an indifference that should
be as absolute as possible. But a cursed voice from
within kept telling me that he was there, too, the
stranger, there in front of me, in the mirror. Waiting like me, with eyes shut. He was there, and I did
not see him. Nor did he see me, since, like me, he
had his eyes closed. But what was he waiting for?
To see me? No. *He could be seen, but could not
see.* He was to me what I was to others; I could be
seen but could not see myself. Yet if I opened my
eyes, would I see *him* like another?

This was the point. How many times, by chance,
had I confronted my eyes in a mirror, with someone who stood looking at me in the same mirror. I
in the mirror did not see myself, but was seen; and

34

the other person, similarly, did not see himself, but saw my face and saw himself being looked at by me. Had I been able to project myself in such a manner as to be able, the I in the mirror, to see myself, I should perhaps have been visible still to the other person, but I—no—I should no longer be able to see him. One could not, at one and the same time, see one's self and see another who stood looking at one in the same mirror.

As I stood thinking these things, with my eyes all the while shut, I put to myself certain questions:

"Is my case any different now, or is it the same? So long as I keep my eyes closed, we are two; I here and he in the mirror. But when I open my eyes, he will turn into me and I into him, and that is the thing I must prevent. I must see him without being seen. Is it possible? As soon as I see him, he will see me, and we will recognize ourselves. No, thanks! I don't want to recognize myself; I want to know him, outside of me. Is it possible? My one supreme effort must be this: not to see myself *in me,* but to be seen *by me,* with my very own eyes, but as if I were another, that other whom all see and I do not. Come, then, be calm, stop every sign of life, and look sharp!"

I opened my eyes. What did I see?

Nothing. I saw *me.* There I was, whipped, burdened with my own thoughts, with a very disgusted countenance. A fierce anger assailed me, and I was tempted to spit in my own face. I held myself in. I smoothed out my wrinkles, did what I could to smother the sharpness of my glance; and lo, even as I smothered it, my image grew pale and seemingly withdrew from me; and I in turn paled and all but fell, and I felt that, had I gone on, I should have been lulled into a doze. I held myself with my eyes. I strove to forestall the feeling that I, likewise, was held by those eyes in front of me— that those eyes, that is to say, were making their way into my own. I did not succeed. I *could feel them*—those eyes. I could see them there, confronting me, but I also could feel them here, in me; I felt them mine, not fixed upon me now but as existing in themselves. And if, for a little, I succeeded in not being thus intimately conscious of them, I did not see them any more. Alas, that was precisely the way it was: I could see them as a part of me, I no longer could see them.

And now, look what happened. As if constrained by this verity which tended to reduce my experiment to a game, my visage suddenly essayed in the mirror an unprepossessing smile.

"Be serious, you imbecile!" I shouted at it then. "There's nothing to laugh about!"

The change of expression in my image was instantaneous, by reason of the spontaneity of my wrath; and this change was followed, with equal suddenness, by a bewildered apathy; as a result of all of which, I succeeded in beholding, there before me in the mirror, my body detached from my imperious soul.

Ah, at last! There it is!

Who was I?

I was nothing. No one. A poor, mortified body, waiting for someone to take it.

"*Moscarda,*" I murmured, after a long silence.

It did not move, but stood gazing at me in astonishment.

It might be that it had another name.

There it was, like a lost dog, without a master and without a name, a dog that one person might call *Flik* and another *Flok,* at his own good pleasure. It did not know anything, not even itself; it lived to live, and did not know how to live; its heart beat, and it did not know it; it breathed, and it did not know it; it moved its eyelids, and was unaware of the fact. I looked at the reddish hair; at the forehead, firm, pale, immobile; at those eyebrows with the circumflex accent; at the greenish eyes, the cornea of which appeared to be perforated here and there with little yellowish spots; astonished, unseeing eyes; that nose which sagged to the right, but handsomely aquiline in contour; the "sandy" mustache hiding the mouth; the firm chin, a trifle prominent.

This is the way it was, you see; they had made it like that, a chip off the old block; it was not for it to be other than what it was, to assume another stature; it might alter in part its aspect, might shave off that mustache, for example; but for the moment it was like this; in time, it would be bald or gray, wrinkled and flabby, toothless; it might incur, too, some disfigurement or other, acquire a glass eye, a wooden leg; but for the moment this was the way it was.

Who was I? Was I, I? But I might also be another! Anyone might be that one there. Might have that reddish hair, those eyebrows with the circumflex accent, and that nose which sagged to the right, not only for me, but likewise for another, who was not I. Why must I, this being, be like this? In life, I had formed for myself no image of myself. Why, then, must I see myself in that body there, why must I see in it an inevitable image of myself?

It stood there before me, as if non-existent, like an apparition out of a dream, that image. And I very readily might fail to recognize myself thus. Supposing, for instance, that I had never seen myself in a mirror? Should I not all the same have had my own thoughts lodged within that stranger's head there? Ah, yes, and how many others? What had my thoughts to do with that hair, hair of that shade, which might not have been there at all any more, or which might have been white or black or blond; or with those greenish eyes, which might equally well have been black or blue, or with that nose, which might have been either straight or pug? I could even very easily feel a profound antipathy for that body, there; and I did feel it.

And yet, all men in summary fashion knew me as that reddish hair, those greenish eyes, and that nose: the whole of that body, which for me was as nothing, mind you, nothing! Each one might take it, that body there, to make of it the Moscarda that he deemed most fitting and that pleased him best, shaping it today in one manner, tomorrow in an-

other, depending upon circumstances and the mood
of the moment. And I, myself— Was I by any
chance acquainted with it? What acquaintance
could I have with it? The moment in which I fixed
it with my gaze, that was all. If I did not wish myself or feel myself to be as I saw myself, then it was
a stranger to me as well, since in addition to those
features which it had, it might have had yet others.
By the time the moment in which I fixed it with
my gaze was past, it was already another; as witness the fact that it was no longer what I had been
as a boy, and was not yet what I should be as an old
man; and here I was today endeavoring to recognize it in the one of yesterday, and so on. And in
that head there, motionless and firm, I might put all
the thoughts I wished, might kindle the most varied
visions, visions such as these: a wood that lies, calm
and mysterious, darkening beneath the light of
stars; a lonely roadstead, wrapped in sickly clouds,
from which a spectral ship slowly weighs anchor at
dawn; a city street swarming with life beneath a
sparkling shower of sun that kindles faces with
purpling gleams and windowpanes, mirrors and the
glass fronts of shops with darting, many-colored
rays of light. I extinguished the vision, and the
head remained there as before, firm and motionless,
in an apathetic astonishment.

Who was that one? No one. A poor body, without a name, waiting for someone to take it.

But all of a sudden, as my thoughts ran like this,
something happened to change my stupor to a loom-
ing terror. I beheld in front of my eyes, through no

will of my own, the apathetically astonished face
of that poor mortified body piteously decomposing,
the nose curling up, the eyes turning over inward,
the lips contracting upward, and the brows drawing
together as if for weeping—they remained like that,
in suspense for an instant, and then without warning came crumbling down, to the explosive accompaniment of a couple of sneezes.   The thing had
happened of itself, at a draught of air from some
place or other, without that poor mortified body's
having said a word to me, and quite beyond any
will of my own.

"To your health!" I cried.

And I beheld in the mirror my first madman's
smile.

VIII

What Then?

THEN, nothing: this. And perhaps you think it is nothing! Following is an initial list of the ruinous reflections and terrible conclusions resulting from the innocent, momentary pleasure that Dida, my wife, had permitted herself. I mean, her calling my attention to the fact that my nose hung down lower on the right side.

REFLECTIONS:

1. *That I was not to others what up to then I had believed that I was to myself;*

2. *That I could not see myself living;*

3. *That, not being able to see myself living, I remained a stranger to myself, that is, one whom others believed they saw and knew, each after his own fashion, but not I;*

4. *That it was impossible to stand this stranger up in front of me, in order to see and know him. I could see myself, but could no longer see him;*

5. *That my body, if I regarded it from without, was like an apparition from a dream, a thing that did not know how to live, but which remained waiting there for someone to take it;*

6. *That, just as I took this my body, to be from time to time what I wished or felt myself to be, so*

41

another similarly might take it, to confer upon it a reality of his own;

7.   *That, finally, this body in itself was so near to being nothing and nobody that a draught of air might cause it to sneeze today and tomorrow might carry it off.*

CONCLUSIONS:

These two for the time being:

1.   *I was beginning to understand at last why it was my wife, Dida, called me Gengè;*

2.   *I made up my mind to find out who I was, at least to those closest to me, acquaintances so-called, and to amuse myself by maliciously decomposing the I that I was to them.*

BOOK SECOND

I

Here I am, and Here Are You

THERE is a point which may be raised against me:

"But how does it come that it never entered your mind, poor deluded Moscarda, that the same thing happens to all the rest that happened to you, that none can see themselves living, and that if you were not to others what up to then you had believed yourself to be, so, in the same manner, others could not have been as you saw them, etc., etc."

My answer is:

It did enter my mind. But I beg your pardon, is it really true that it entered your minds as well? I have been willing to suppose it, but I do not believe it. I moreover believe that if, in reality, such a thought had entered your minds, and had taken root there as it took root in my mind, every one of you would have committed the same follies that I committed.

Be sincere. The thought never passed through your heads that you would like to see yourselves living. You are bent upon living for your own sakes, and you are wise in so doing, without giving yourselves a thought of what, in the meanwhile, you may be to others; not, in fact, that the opinion of others does not matter to you—it matters very much indeed; it is rather because you are under the blissful illusion that others, from without, must picture you to themselves as you picture yourselves. And accordingly, should someone call your attention to the fact that your nose sags a little to the right—it doesn't?—that yesterday you told a lie—nothing of the sort?— Oh, come, a very little one, of no consequence— In short, if on certain occasions you become barely conscious of not being to others the same individual that you are to yourselves, what do you do? (Be sincere.) You do nothing, or very little. You make up your minds, in the long run, with an admirable and utter sureness of yourselves, that others have misunderstood you, misjudged you, and that is that. If it is a matter of concern to you, you seek to correct that judgment by giving clarifying explanations; if it is not a matter of concern, you let it go and shrug your shoulders, exclaiming, "Oh, well, my conscience is clear, and that suffices me."

Isn't that the way it is?

I beg your pardon, my good people. You have just had a big word in your mouths; permit me now to insert a tiny, tiny thought in your minds. This thought: that your conscience, here, has nothing to do with the case. I shall not say that it is worth nothing, if it means everything to you; I shall say, to please you, that I similarly have my own, and know that it is worth nothing. Do you know why? Because I know, there is your conscience, too. Ah, yes. And so very different from mine. Excuse me, if I talk for a moment like the philosophers. Is your conscience, by any means, something absolute, that

may suffice to itself? If we were solitary beings, it
might be so. But in that case, my good friends, it
would not be conscience. Unfortunately, here I am,
and here are you. Unfortunately. And what does
it mean, then, that you have your conscience, and
that it suffices you? That others may think of you
and judge you as they please, that is, unjustly, because you all the while are safe in the comforting
assurance that you have done no wrong?   Come,
come, I beg you: and is it not others who give you
that very assurance, that selfsame comfort?

It is you yourselves, is it? And how does that
come?

Ah, I know how: through that obstinate belief
you hold that, if others had been in your place and
had understood your case as it was, they would all
have acted exactly as you did, would have done
neither more nor less than you did. Excellent! But
upon what do you base that assertion? I know the
answer to that question, too, eh? Upon certain abstract and general principles, upon which, abstractly
and generally, which means aside from concrete and
particular cases in life, it is possible for all to agree
(at a very slight cost). Yet how does it come, meanwhile, that all condemn you, or fail to approve you,
or even deride you? It is obvious that they are
unable to recognize, as you do, those same general
principles, in the particular case that concerns you,
or to recognize themselves in the action which you
have performed.

For what is it, then, that your conscience suffices

you? For enabling you to feel alone? Good heavens, no. Solitude terrifies you. What do you thereupon do? You picture to yourselves any number of heads, all like your own. Any number of heads that are also your own. And these heads, at a given signal, drawn out from you as by an invisible wire, say yes and no, and no and yes, to you, as you would have them say. All of which comforts you and gives you a feeling of security.

It is a splendid game you have there, that of the self-sufficing conscience.

II

And Then?

Do you know, on the contrary, the basis upon which
the whole thing rests? 1 will tell you. Upon a presumption that God keeps you ever. The presumption
that reality, as it is for you, ought to be and is the
same for all others. You go on living inside it; you
walk out of it in security. You see it, you touch it;
and within it, you even smoke a cigar, if you like
(a pipe? very well, a pipe), and blissfully stay there
watching the smoke-spirals vanishing, one by one,
in the air. Without the faintest suspicion that all
the reality about you has for others no more consistency than has that smoke.

You say no? Look. I was living with my wife in
the house that my father had had built after my
mother's premature death, because he wished to
move out of the one in which he had lived with her,
which was full of harrowing memories. I was a lad
at the time, and it was not until later that I became
fully aware that this house, down to the last, had
been left unfinished by my father and practically
open to anyone who chose to enter. That archway
for a door, without a door, which rose, on one side
and the other, by the whole of its central span,
above the unfinished walls of the huge front courtyard, with the sill beneath destroyed and the

pilasters peeling off at the corners—all this makes me think now that my father possibly left it so, empty and up in the air, one might say, for the reason that he believed the house after his death would necessarily remain my property, which is equivalent to saying, the property of all and of none, and that it would, accordingly, have been useless to repair a door.

So long as my father lived, no one attempted to set foot in that courtyard. Ever so many hewed stones had been left lying about; and the first thought of any passer-by might well have been that work had been stopped for a while but would shortly be resumed. But no sooner had the grass begun shooting up between the pebbles and along the walls than those useless stones seemed, of a sudden, old and crumbling. In the course of time, my father having died, they came to furnish seats for the gossips of the neighborhood, who, hesitatingly at first, one after the other, at last got up their courage to cross the threshold, in search it seemed of a place where they might repair to find a seat, silence, and a bit of grateful shade; after which, seeing that no one said anything, they left it to their hens to hesitate for a little while longer, and forthwith proceeded to look upon as their own that courtyard and the water that sprang up from the basin in the center; they would do their washing there and hang out their clothes to dry; and with the merry, dazzling sun over all that white expanse of sheets and shirts that fluttered from the lines, they would let down their hair, glossy with oil, over their shoulders, to "have a hunt" in their heads as the monkeys do.

I never manifested either annoyance or pleasure at this invasion of theirs, although I was especially irritated by the sight of one continually prying old hag with dried-up eyes and with the hump on her back plainly outlined under her faded green doublet, and my stomach was turned by a fat, filthy and tattered wretch with a horrifying pap always sticking out from her bosom, while on her knees she held a grimy brat with an overgrown, disgustingly scurvy head, the scabs of which were visible among the reddish mop. My wife, I fancy, profited somewhat from leaving them there, since she made use of them at need, giving them by way of compensation either the left-overs from the kitchen or a few cast-off garments.

Pebble-paved like the street, the courtyard was wholly sloping. I can see myself as a lad, on vacation from boarding school, standing late of an evening on one of the balconies of the house, which was then new. What a boundless pain I felt at sight of the great livid whiteness of all those pebbles on the side of the slope, with that big basin in the middle, mysteriously sonorous! Rust by that time had almost eaten away the red-tinted varnish of the iron haft which at the top regulates the pulley over which the well-rope runs; how sad it seemed to me, that faded hue of varnish on that sickly looking iron haft! Sick, too, perhaps, from the melancholy squeaking of the pulley, when the wind of a night stirred the rope; while over the deserted courtyard was the white splendor of the starry sky, starry but veiled, a sky which in that vain, white, dusty splendor seemed fixed up there forever.

Upon my father's death, Quantorzo, charged with looking after my affairs, thought of closing off with a partition the rooms which my father had reserved for his own dwelling, and of making out of them a small apartment to let. My wife was not opposed to this. And into that apartment there came to live, shortly afterward, a very silent and thoughtful old man, always very well dressed, cleanly and simply, a little old man but with something of the soldier in his slender well-set-up figure, as well as in his energetic face, somewhat scarred by time, which was that of a retired colonel. On either side of his face, like samples of calligraphy, he had a perfect fishlike eye, while his cheeks were a dense network of violet-colored veins. I had never paid any attention to him, nor cared to know who he was or how he lived. I had met him several times on the stair, and hearing him say, very courteously, "Good morning," or "Good evening," I had jumped to the conclusion that this housemate of mine was a very courteous individual.

No suspicion was awakened in me by a complaint of his concerning the gnats that molested him at night, and which, in his opinion, came from the big warehouses, to the right of the dwelling, that had been converted by Quantorzo (all this after my father's death) into filthy coachhouses which were rented out.

"Ah, really!" I had exclaimed upon that occasion, in response to his complaint.

But I remember perfectly that in this exclamation of mine there was a note of displeasure, not assuredly over the gnats which were molesting my tenant, but over those clean airy warehouses which, as a boy, I had seen being built, and where I used to run about, finding a strange exaltation in the dazzling whiteness of the plaster and something like a drunkenness in the cool humidity of the factory, over the resounding brick pavement, still all sprinkled over with chalk. In the light of the sun which came in through the big iron-grated windows, one had to shut one's eyes, as if the very walls were on fire.

Nevertheless, those coach-houses with their old landaus for hire and their three-horse turnouts, though they might be wholly saturated with the foul odor of rotting litters and with the grime from repeated rinsings that lay stagnating out in front, also made me think of the gladness I had known upon carriage excursions as a boy, when we would go for an outing, down the high street and out into the open country, which impressed me as having been made to receive and diffuse the music of horses' bells. And in gratitude for this memory, it seemed to me that the proximity of the coach-houses might be tolerated, all the more so by reason of the fact that, quite apart from the coach-houses, it was known that gnats caused much annoyance at Richieri, and every household commonly employed mosquito-netting.

What impression must have been made upon my neighbor and tenant by the sight of a smile upon my lips, as he with his ferocious little face shouted at me that he never could endure netting, because it made him feel as if he were smothering? That smile of mine assuredly was expressive of astonishment and compassion. Not to be able to endure netting, when I should have gone on using it, even if all the gnats in Richieri had disappeared, owing to the delight it gave me, stretched as I stretched it, sky-high, and draped all about the bed without a fold. The room that one sees and does not see, through that myriad of little holes in the light tulle; the isolated bed; the impression of being wrapped in a white cloud.

I did not take any account of what he might think of me after this meeting. I continued seeing him on the stairs and hearing him say, "Good morning" or "Good evening"—and was left with the idea that he was an exceedingly courteous fellow indeed. I assure you, on the contrary, that at the very moment when he, with outward courtesy, was saying to me on the stair, "Good morning" or "Good evening," he was making me live inside himself as a perfect imbecile, for the reason that I tolerated the invasion of the old women out there in the court, and because of the impinging wash-house stench and the gnats.

Obviously, I should not have gone on thinking, "Dear me, what a courteous chap my housemate is," had I been able to see myself inside him, while he, on the other hand, saw me as I should never have been able to see myself, by which I mean from without, in my stead, but still within that vision of his own which he at that time had of men and things, and in which he made me live after his own fashion: as a perfect imbecile. I did not know it, but kept on thinking, "Dear me, what a courteous chap my housemate is—"

III

With Your Permission

THERE is a knock at the door of your room.

And yet, you remain where you are, remained stretched out comfortably in your easy chair. I will sit here. You say no?

"Why?"

Ah, that is the chair in which, all these many years ago, your poor mother died. If you don't mind my saying so, you would not have given a penny for it, but now you would not sell it for all the money in the world; I can well believe that. Any one, meanwhile, who saw it in your well-furnished room would certainly, if he did not know the facts in the case, wonder how you could go on keeping it here, old, faded and torn as it is.

These are your chairs. And this is a tiny table, as tiny as could be. That is a window, looking out over the garden. And out there are the pines, the cypresses.

I know. Delightful hours spent in this room, which to you is so beautiful, with a glimpse of those cypresses yonder. Yet on account of this room, you have broken off with the friend who used to come to see you almost every day. and who now not only does not come any more, but who goes about telling everybody that you are mad, quite mad, to go on living in a house like this.

"With all those cypresses in a row out in front," he goes about saying. "Why, my good people, there are more than a score of cypresses; it's like a cemetery."

He cannot get over it.

You blink your eyes and shrug your shoulders.

"A matter of taste," you sigh.

For it does seem to you that it is, properly speaking, a question of taste, of opinion or of habit; and you do not for a moment doubt the reality of these beloved objects, a reality which it gives you pleasure to see and to touch. But go away from this house, come back in three or four years to view it again, in another frame of mind than the one you are in today, and you will find that there is nothing left of that reality which you so cherish.

"Oh, look, so this is the room? And this the garden?"

And let us hope in the name of heaven that some other one near of kin to you has not died, so that to you now all those cypresses there take on the appearance of a cemetery. You tell me that this is something everybody knows, that the mind changes and anyone may be mistaken. It is, in fact, an old story. I, however, do not pretend to be telling you anything new. I merely have a question to put to you:

"Good Lord, why is it, then, that you act as if you did not know it? Why is it that you insist upon believing that the only reality is your own, the reality of today, and why do you cry out in angry astonishment that your friend is wrong, although he, poor chap, whatever he might do, could never have within himself the mind that is your own?"

IV

Begging Your Pardon Once Again

LET me say one thing more, and have done with it.

I do not wish to offend you. You speak of your conscience. You do not care to have any doubt cast upon it. Excuse me, I had forgotten. Yet I recognize the fact, I must recognize it, that to yourself, within yourself, you are not as I, from without, see you. There is no ill-will in the matter. I would have you be persuaded at least of this. You know yourself, feel yourself, will yourself in a fashion that is not mine, but yours; and once again, you believe that yours is right and mine is wrong. It may be so, I am not saying it isn't. But can your fashion be mine, and vice-versa?

Suppose we go back and start at the beginning? I can believe everything that you tell me. I do believe it. I am offering you a chair; sit down, and let us see if we cannot agree upon this. After something like an hour of good conversation, we shall understand each other perfectly. Tomorrow, you will come to me with your hands to your face, crying: "How does it happen? What did you mean? Didn't you tell me so-and-so?"

Quite right, I did tell you so-and-so. The unfortunate part is that you, my dear friend, will never know, and I shall never be able to tell you, how what you say to me is translated inside me. You did not speak Turkish, no. We both employed, you and I, the same language, the same words. But is it our fault, yours and mine, if words in themselves are empty? Empty, my dear friend. You fill them with your meaning, as you speak them to me; while I, in taking them in, inevitably fill them with my own. We thought we understood each other; we did not understand each other at all.

Another old story, eh? Something everybody knows. I do not pretend to be telling you anything new; I merely have a question to put to you:

"Good Lord, why is it then that you insist upon acting as if you did not know it? Why do you insist upon speaking to me of yourself, if you know that, in order to be to me what you are to yourself, and in order for me to be to you what I am to myself, it would be necessary for me, inside myself, to confer upon you that same reality which you confer upon yourself, all of which is impossible? For alas, dear friend, whatever you do, you will always confer upon me a reality after your own manner, believing still that it is my manner; and it may be, I do not say that it isn't; it is altogether likely that it is; but it is a 'my manner' of which I know nothing and never can know anything; it is only you, who see me from without, that can know it; hence, a 'my manner' for you, not a 'my manner' for me.

"If there were only outside of us, for you and for me—if there were only a Mrs. My-Reality and a Mrs. Your-Reality, I mean self-existent, unvarying, immutable. There isn't. There is in me and for me a reality that is mine: that which I confer upon myself; a reality that is yours, in you and for you: that which you confer upon yourself; and these are never the same, either for me or for you."

"And then?"

"Then, my friend, we must console ourselves with this reflection: that mine is no truer than yours, and that they endure for but a moment, both yours and mine.

"Is your head swimming a little? Then, then—let's leave off."

V

Fixations

WELL, then, I am coming to this, that you ought not to say that any more—you ought not to say that you have your conscience, and that it suffices you.

When did you do that thing? Yesterday, today, a minute ago? And now? Ah, you yourself are now disposed to admit that you might conceivably have acted differently. And why? Good heavens, but you're pale! So even you are now beginning to realize that, a minute ago, *you were a different person?*

Ah, yes, ah, yes, my dear friend, think it over well: a minute ago, when this thing happened to you, you were a different person; not only that, you were at the same time a hundred others, a hundred-thousand. And believe me, there is no occasion for wonderment in this fact. Look rather and see if it now seems to you so certain that tomorrow you will be what you assume you are today.

My dear friend, the truth is this: they are all fixations. Today, you fix yourself in one fashion, tomorrow in another. I shall proceed to tell you how and why.

VI

I Am Telling You Now

HAVE you ever seen a house in process of construction? I have, many times, here at Richieri. And I thought:

"Just look for a moment at man, what he is capable of doing! He mutilates the mountain, hews rocks out of it, squares them, lays them one upon another, and, what is and is not, that which was a bit of the mountain has become a house."

" 'I,' says the mountain, 'am a mountain and do not move.'

"So you do not move, old girl? Just look at those ox-drawn carts. They are laden with you, with your stones. They are carting you off in little wagons, my dear! Did you think you were going to stay where you are? Already, you are a couple of miles away, down on the plain. Where? Why, in those houses there—don't you see them?—a yellow one, a red one, a white one, of two, three and four stories. And your beeches, your walnuts, your firs—there they are, in my house. Do you see how well we have worked them over? Who would recognize them now in those chairs, in those clothespresses, in those cupboards?

"You, mountain, are so very much bigger than man, with your beeches, your walnuts and your firs; man is a very small animal, and yet, he has in him-

63

self something that you have not. From standing always on his feet, that is to say, upright on two paws only, he grew tired; to stretch out on the earth like the other animals did not appeal to his sense of comfort and was not good for him, especially since, having lost his hair, his hide—his hide, eh!—had become more delicate. It was then that his eyes fell upon the tree, and the thought occurred to him that he might be able to get out of it something upon which he could more conveniently sit. He then perceived that the raw wood was not comfortable and he padded it; he thereupon flayed his domestic animals, while others he sheared, and proceeded to line the wood with leather, while the space between the leather and the wood he stuffed with wool.

"‘Ah!’ he murmured, as he stretched himself out, 'how comfortable this is!'

"The goldfinch sings in its cage between the curtains upon the window-shelf. Can it be that it is conscious of the approaching springtime? Ah, it may be that the nearness of the spring is similarly felt by the old walnut bough from which my chair was made, which now creaks to the goldfinch's song. And it may further be that, by means of the song and the creaking, the imprisoned goldfinch and the walnut made into a chair understand each other."

VII

What Does the House Have to Do With It?

IT MAY appear to you that all this talk about the house has nothing to do with the case, for the reason that you now see your house as it is, among the others that go to make up the town. You see about you your furnishings, those which you, in accordance with your taste and your means, have seen fit to acquire for your convenience. And they exhale about you a dear, familiar comfort, animated as they are by all your memories; they are no longer objects, but, in a manner, intimate parts of yourself, in which you can touch and feel what impresses you as being the assured reality of your existence. Whether they be of beech, of walnut or of fir, your furnishings, embodying the memories of your fireside intimacy, are impregnated with the special atmosphere that lingers in every house, and which gives to our lives something that is almost an odor, one that makes itself felt all the more strongly at a distance; which is to say, that no sooner do we enter another house than we are at once aware of a different atmosphere.

It annoys you, I can see, my having called you back to the beeches, the walnuts and the mountain firs. It is as if you already were becoming a trifle infected with my madness, since at everything I tell you, your face at once clouds as you inquire, "Why? What does that have to do with it?"

VIII

Out into the Open

COME, now, you need not be afraid that I am going to
wreck either your furniture, your peace or your
love of home.

Air! Air! Let us leave the house, leave the town.
I am not saying that you can put any too much confidence in me; but come, do not be afraid. Come
with me to where the street with its houses breaks
into the open country.

Yes, this is a street. Are you really afraid that I
may tell you it is not? Street, street. A flint-stone
street: look out for the flints. And those are lamp-
posts. Come on; you are safe.

Ah, those distant sky-blue mountains! I say "sky-
blue"; and you, too, say "sky-blue," do you not? We
agree. And that near one there, with the chestnut
grove—they *are* chestnuts, aren't they?—do you see
how we agree?—of the cupuliferous family, with a
tall trunk. *Castagno marrone.*[1] What a huge plain
down there ("green," eh? for you and for me, it is
"green"; we will say that it is; how marvellously well
we understand each other); and in those meadows
yonder, look, look, what a blaze of red poppies in the
sun!—How is that? Red babies' hoods? — Well,
well, I must be blind! Right you are, red woolen

---

[1] *Castagno* and *marrone* are the two Italian terms for chestnut, the
marrone being the larger variety.

hoods. They looked like poppies to me. And yet, that red cravat of yours— How pleasant it is out here in the blue and the green, in the cool sunlit air of the open spaces! So you are doffing that old felt hat, are you? What, perspiring already? Well, you are fairly stout, you know, Lord bless you! If you could see the little black and white squares on the seat of your trousers— Come, off with your coat! You can do without it.

The country! A restful change, eh, this peace? You feel yourself relaxing. Very good; but can you tell me where it is? I mean, peace. No, no, don't be afraid! Does it really seem to you that peace is to be found here? Let us understand each other, for heaven's sake! Let us not do anything to spoil our perfect agreement. All that I see here, if you will permit me to say so, is the thing of which I am conscious in myself at this moment, a tremendous sottishness, that renders your face, and my own as well no doubt, those of a pair of blessed idiots, but which we attribute to the earth and to the plants, since they appear to live for the sake of living, and could only go on living in such a sottishness as this.

Let us say, then, that what we call peace is to be found within ourselves. Doesn't it seem so to you? And do you know where it comes from? From the very simple fact that we have just now left the town, that is, a world that is *built*—houses, streets, churches, squares—not for this reason alone, however, because it is *built*, but also because we no longer live for the sake of living, like these plants, without knowing how to live, but rather for something that is not and which we put there, for something that gives meaning and value to life, a meaning, a value which here, at least in part, we succeed in losing, or of which we recognize the grievous vanity. Hence comes your languor and your melancholy. I understand, I understand. Let-down of nerves. Afflicting need of self-abandonment. You feel yourself relaxing, you abandon yourself.

IX

Clouds and Wind

Aʜ, to be no longer conscious of being, like a stone, like a plant! To remember no longer even one's own name! Stretched out upon the grass, hands interlaced at the back of one's neck, to look up at the dazzling, sun-puffed clouds as they sail past in the blue sky, to listen to the wind which makes, up there in the chestnut grove, a sound like the breaking of the sea.

Clouds and wind.

What did you say? Alas, alas! Clouds? Wind? And does it not seem to you indeed everything, to take cognizance of and recognize the fact that those objects which go sailing so luminously through that boundless sky-blue void are clouds? Does the cloud by any chance know anything of the fact of being? Neither do the tree and the rock know anything of the cloud, nor even of themselves; they are wrapped in their loneliness.

Taking cognizance of and recognizing the cloud, you may, my good friends, think of the change that water (and why not?) undergoes, which becomes clouds to become again water. A fine thing, that. And any sorry little physics instructor can explain to you the change that takes place. But to explain the wherefore of the why?

X

The Bird

LISTEN, listen: up there in the chestnut grove, blows
of an ax. Down there in the quarry, blows of the
pick.

To mutilate the mountain, to fell trees for building houses. Down there, in the old town, other
houses. Drudgery, anxiety, hardships of every
sort: why? To come to a ridge, my good people,
and then to cause to issue from that ridge a little
smoke that is speedily dispersed in the emptiness
of space.

Every thought, every memory of man is like that
smoke.

We are in the country here; languor has relaxed
our limbs; it is natural that illusions and disillusion-
ments, joys and griefs, hopes and desires should
appear to us vain and transitory in the presence of
that sentiment which breathes from objects that
are enduring, self-overcoming, impassive. All you
have to do is to look at those tall mountains over
yonder, on the other side of the valley, far, far away,
smoky on the horizon, airy in the sunset, wrapped
in a roseate mist.

What happens now? Stretched out at ease, you
hurl your old felt hat up into the air; and you be-

come almost tragic, as you exclaim, "Oh, the ambitions of mankind!" Quite right. For example, that cry of victory because man, like that old hat of yours, has started to fly, to play the bird! Meanwhile, have a look at a real bird here, and see how it flies. Did you see it? A more honest, more graceful facility, accompanied by a spontaneous trill of joy. Think, on the other hand, of the awkward, rumbling apparatus, and of all the fear, anxiety and mortal anguish of man when he tries to play the bird! Here a swish of wings and a trill; there a noisy, foul-smelling motor, and death in the offing. The motor goes wrong, the motor stops; good-bye, birdie!

"Ah, man," you say, as you lie there, stretched out upon the grass, "let him fly, if he wants to! Why should you want to fly? When did you ever fly?"

Noble words. You say that here and now, because you are in the country, stretched out upon the grass. But rise up and go back to town, and no sooner will you be there than you shall at once understand why it is man wants to fly. Here, my good friends, you have seen the real bird, which really flies, and you have lost sight of the meaning and value of invented wings and mechanic flight. You will quickly re-acquire it there, where all is invented and mechanical, assembling and construction, a world within a world, a manufactured, agglomerate, adjusted world, a world of twisted artifice, of adaptation, and of vanity, a world that has a meaning and a value solely by reason of the fact that man is its artificer.

Come, come; let me give you a hand to help you up. You are stout, you know. Wait, there's a blade or two of grass on your back— There; let's be on our way.

XI

Back to Town

JUST look, will you, at those trees which, in a row to the right and left of the sidewalk, border our Corsa di Porta Vecchia; how lost they appear to be, poor city trees, all clipped and combed!

It is altogether likely that trees do not think and that animals do not reason. But merciful heavens, if trees did think, and if they could talk, who knows what they would say, the poor things, planted as we have planted them in the midst of the town, to provide us with a little shade! It would seem, as they view their reflections in these shop windows, that they were asking what it is they are doing here, amid all these bustling people, in the clamorous confusion of city life. Set out all these many years ago, they have remained wretched and unkempt dwarfs. They give no sign of having any ears; but who knows? it may be that trees, in order to grow properly, have need of silence all the same.

Have you ever been in the little Olivella Square, outside the walls, at the old White Trinitarian monastery? What a dreamlike atmosphere of abandonment in that little square, and what a weird silence when, from the dark musk-scented tiles of that old cloister, the morning's blue, blue infant smile appears! And yet, each year, the earth there, in its stupid maternal ingenuity, seeks to take advantage of that silence. Possibly, it fancies that the town is no longer present, that men have deserted this little square, and accordingly endeavors to take possession of it again by reaching out, very softly, very gently, innumerable tendrils of grass above the pavement. Nothing could be more fresh and delicate than those timid slender shoots, with which the whole of the little square will soon be verdant. But unfortunately, it will not last more than a month. The town is there, and it is not permitted grass blades to sprout. Four or five street cleaners come every year, squat down on the ground, and proceed to grub it up with their iron implements.

I saw there last year a couple of little birds which, hearing the grating of those implements on the scraggy gray stones of the pavement, flew from the hedge to the convent eaves and from there back to the hedge, wagging their tiny heads with sidelong glances, as if in anxious inquiry as to what those men could be doing there.

"And don't you see, little birdies," I said to them, "don't you see what they are doing? They are trimming this old pavement's beard."

They flew away in horror, those two little birds. Happy those who have wings and can fly away! How many other animals have not, but are taken, shut up and domesticated in the city and even in the country; and how sad a thing is their forced obedience to man's strange needs! What do they understand of it all? They draw the cart, they pull the plow.

But perhaps they, too, animals, plants and all

things, know a meaning and a value of their own, one which man is unable to grasp, shut up as he is in those which he himself gives to one and all, and which Nature very often, for her part, declines to recognize and ignores. It would be well, if there were a little more understanding between man and Nature. Too often, Nature takes a pleasure in knocking down all our ingenious constructions. Cyclones, earthquakes— But man does not give up. He rebuilds, rebuilds, stubborn little animal that he is. Everything to him is material for building. For the reason that he has in himself that something, a stranger to itself, which impels him to build, and to transform after his own fashion the raw material which ignorant and, when she chooses to be, perhaps patient Nature offers him. If he would only be content with taking things that, until better proof is adduced, are not known to possess the faculty of suffering torture by reason of our adaptations and constructions! But not so, my good people. Man takes even himself as material, and builds himself, my dear sirs, like a house.

Do you think you can know yourself, if you do not in some fashion build yourself up? Or that I can know you, if I do not build you up after my own fashion? Or you me, if you do not build me up after your fashion? We can only know that to which we succeed in giving form. Yet what can there be in the way of knowledge? Can it be that this form is the thing itself? Yes, as much for me as for you, but not for me as it is for you; so true is this that I do not recognize myself in that form which you confer upon me, nor you yourself in that which I confer upon you; the same thing is not the same to all; and even for any one of us, it may constantly change, and in fact does constantly so change. And yet, there is no reality beyond the one which lies in that momentary form which we succeed in conferring upon ourselves, upon others, upon things. The reality that I hold for you lies in the form that you confer upon me, but it is reality to you and not to me; the reality that you hold for me lies in the form that I confer upon you, but it is reality to me and not to you; and for myself, I have no other reality than that which I succeed in conferring upon myself. And how is that? Why, by building myself up, that is all.

So you think, do you, it is only houses that are built? I am continually building myself and building you, and you are doing the same, inversely. And the construction lasts so long as the material of our emotions does not crumble, and so long as the cement of our will holds firm. Why do you think it is, otherwise, that firmness of will and constancy of feeling are so highly commended to you? Let the will waver but a little, let the emotions alter by a hair's-breadth, undergo ever so slight a change, and it is good-bye to reality as we know it! We at once become aware that it was nothing other than an illusion on our part.

Firmness of will, then, constancy of feeling. Hold fast, hold fast, if you do not care to take these dives in the void, and go forth to meet unwelcome surprises.

But what fine buildings come out of it all.

XII

That Dear Gengè

"No, no, my darling, be quiet! Do you mean to imply that I do not know what is pleasing and what is displeasing to you? I know your tastes very well, indeed, and your way of thinking."

How many times had Dida, my wife, said this to me? And I, imbecile that I was, had never taken any notice of it. Yet no doubt she knew that Gengè of hers better than I knew him! Seeing it was she who had built him up! And he was not by any means a puppet. If any one, the puppet was I.

Domination? Substitution? Well, hardly! To dominate someone, it is necessary that the someone exist; and it is equally necessary that he exist, and that it be possible to take him by the shoulders and pull him backward, if one is to make a substitution and put another in his place. Dida, my wife, had neither dominated me nor made a substitution. It would, on the contrary, have seemed to her a domination and an act of substitution, if I, growing rebellious and affirming in any manner a will to be after my own fashion, had snatched that Gengè of hers off his feet.

For that Gengè of hers existed, while I for her did not exist at all, never had existed. My reality for her lay in that Gengè of hers that she had fashioned, a being with thoughts, tastes and emotions that

77

were not mine, and which I should never have been able to alter in the slightest degree, without running the risk of becoming at once another being whom she would not have recognized, a stranger, whom she would not have been able any longer either to understand or to love.

It is only too true that I had never been able to give any sort of form to my life; I never had firmly willed myself after a special fashion of my own, either for the reason that I never had encountered obstacles which might have aroused in me a will to resistance and to self-affirmation, of one kind or another, with regard to others and to myself, or else on account of my mental disposition to think and feel the very contrary of what I had thought and felt a short while before, a disposition, that is, to decompose and disperse in myself, by means of assiduous and often contradictory reflections, any mental or sentimental formation; or lastly, it may have been because my nature was one that was prone to yield, to abandon itself to the discretion of others, not so much out of weakness as out of nonchalance and an anticipatory resignation to such vexations as might come to me as a result of it all.

And now, just see what had come to me! The fact was, I did not know myself, did not possess for myself any reality of my own, but was in a state of constant semi-fluid, semi-malleable fusion; others knew me, each after his own fashion, in accordance with that reality which they had conferred upon me; which is to say, they saw in me a Moscarda that was not I, inasmuch as I, properly speaking, was no one to myself; there were as many Moscardas as there were other individuals, and all of them were more real than I, who had, I repeat, no reality whatsoever so far as I myself was concerned.

Gengè, yes, he did have, for my wife, Dida. I could find no sort of consolation in this, however, for the reason, I assure you, that it would have been difficult to imagine a sillier creature than this, my wife Dida's dear Gengè. The amusing part, incidentally, is that her Gengè was not by any means without faults in her eyes. But she forgave him all! There were any number of things about him that did not please her; for she had not built him up altogether after her own fashion, in accordance with her own taste; no. After whose fashion, then? Certainly, not after mine; for I repeat, I could not bring myself to recognize as my own the thoughts, tastes and emotions which she attributed to her Gengè. It is obvious, then, that the reason she attributed these to him was that Gengè, as she saw him, possessed those tastes and thought and felt that way after *his* fashion, which comes near to saying, really *his,* in accordance with *his* reality, which was not as a matter of fact *mine.*

I saw her weeping sometimes over certain griefs which he, Gengè, had caused her. Yes, my dear sirs, he! And if I asked her, "But why, dear?" she would reply, "So you have to ask, do you? I suppose it was not enough, what you said to me just now!"

"I?"

"Yes, you, you!"

"But when in the name of goodness was it? And what was it?"

I was amazed. It was plain that the meaning which I gave to my words was one thing for me, and that the meaning which those words, become Gengè's, assumed for her was quite another thing. Certain words which, spoken by me or by another, would not have caused her any sorrow, when uttered by Gengè made her weep, since in Gengè's mouth they assumed a different and to me unknown value; they made her weep, yes, my dear sirs, they did.

I, therefore, spoke for myself alone, while she held converse with her Gengè. And the latter replied to her through my mouth in a manner of which I remained wholly ignorant. And it is incredible how silly, false and meaningless all the things became that I said to her and which she repeated to me.

"But what do you mean?" I would ask her. "Did I say anything like that?"

"Yes, Gengè, dear, you did say exactly that!"

Now mind you, those were her Gengè's silly remarks; but they were not silly remarks; quite the contrary! It was Gengè's way of thinking, that. And I— Ah!— how I should have liked to box his ears, to give him a caning, tear him to pieces! But I could not come at him. For the reason that, notwithstanding the displeasures which he caused her, the silly things he said, Gengè was greatly loved by my wife, Dida; he lived up for her, as he was, to the ideal of a good husband, in whom one may over-look a few trifling faults out of gratitude for all his other good qualities. And if I did not want Dida, my wife, to go looking for her ideal in another, I must not lay hands upon her Gengè.

At first, I thought it might be because my emotions were too complicated, my thoughts too abstruse, my tastes too out of the ordinary, and that for this reason my wife, failing frequently to comprehend them, proceeded to disguise them. I felt, in short, that my ideas and my emotions could not be understood, unless reduced to the size of that little head and heart, and that my tastes could not possibly fall in with her simplicity. But what was I thinking of, what was I thinking of! She was not disguising them; she was not reducing my thoughts and feelings. No, no. So disguised, so reduced, as they came to her from Gengè's mouth, my wife, Dida, thought them silly—even she, you under-stand? And who did, then, thus disguise and re-duce them? Why, the reality that was Gengè, my good people! Gengè, as she had fashioned him for herself, could not have any other than those thoughts, those feelings, those tastes. He was a big silly, but a little dear. Ah, yes, how very dear to her! She loved him like that: silly dear. And she really did love him.

I was afforded so many proofs of it. This one will do, the first that comes to mind. Dida, from the time she was a girl, had been in the habit of combing her hair in a certain way that not only pleased her, but me as well, very much. No sooner was she married than she changed her way of combing her hair. While permitting her to do as she saw fit, I told her that this new way did not please me in the least. When, lo and behold, she one morning appeared suddenly in her dressing gown, with the comb still in her hand, her hair done up in the old way, and very red in the face.

"Gengè!" she cried, as she threw open the door and stood upon the threshold to give me a view of her; she burst into a laugh as she did so. I was all admiration, fairly dazzled.

"So!" I exclaimed, "at last!"

But she at once ran her hands through her hair, jerked out the combs, and undid in an instant the whole of her headdress.

"Be off with you!" she said. "I was only playing a joke on you. I know very well, Mr. Smarty, that you don't like my hair combed that way!"

I broke in, protestingly.

"But who told you that, Dida, dear? I swear to you that, on the contrary—"

She stopped my mouth with her hand.

"Be off with you!" she repeated. "You are just saying that to please me. But it is not my own pleasure that I should be thinking of, my dear. Do you mean to tell me that I don't know what my Gengè likes best?"

And with this, she ran away.

Do you get it? It was as certain as certain could be that her Gengè liked her hair better combed that other way, and so, she combed it that way, which was pleasing neither to her nor to me. But it pleased her Gengè, and she sacrificed herself. You say, that does not mean much? Are not such as these true and real sacrifices for a woman?

She loved him so! And I—now that all at last was cleared up for me—began to be terribly jealous —not of myself, believe me, please; I know you feel like laughing—not of myself, good people, but of one that was not I, of an imbecile who had intruded himself between me and my wife, not like an empty shadow, no—believe me, please—because he rather made an empty shadow of me—yes, me—by appropriating my body to win her love.

Think it over well. Was not my wife, perhaps, kissing upon my lips one that was not I? Upon my lips? No! What do you mean, mine! To what extent were they *mine*, really *mine*, those lips she kissed? Was it, perchance, my body that she held in her arms? But to what extent could that body *really* be mine, to what extent could it *really* belong to me, if I was not the one that she embraced and loved? Think it over well. Should you not feel that you were being betrayed by your wife, with the most refined sort of perfidy, if there were a means of your knowing that, even as she clasped you in her arms, she was relishing and enjoying, through the medium of your body, the embrace of another whom she held in her mind and heart? Very well, then; how did my case differ from that? My case was even worse! For in the one that we have supposed, your wife—begging your pardon— while in your embrace is merely picturing to herself the embrace of another, whereas in my case, my wife was actually clasping in her arms the reality of one that was not I!

And he was so very real, this one, that when, in exasperation, I wished to destroy him, by imposing in place of his a reality of my own, my wife, who had not been my wife but his wife, was at once horror-struck, as if she had found herself in a stranger's arms, the arms of a man she did not know; and she declared that she could not love me any more, that she could not go on living with me, not even for a minute longer; and she ran away.

Yes, good people, as you shall see, she ran away.

BOOK THIRD

I

Forced Madness

BUT I want to tell you first, briefly at any rate, of the mad things I began to do, by way of discovering all those other Moscardas that went on living in my nearest acquaintances, and with the object of destroying them one by one.

Forced madness. For having never thought, up to that time, of constructing for myself a Moscarda who, in my eyes and according to my reckoning, would represent a mode of being that to me was seemingly distinguished as belonging to me and me alone, I accordingly found it impossible—and this should not be hard to understand—to act with any sort of logical consistency. I deemed it necessary, from time to time, to prove myself the contrary of the being that I was, or whom I supposed myself to be, in this acquaintance or that, after I had exerted myself to comprehend the reality which they had conferred upon me: impoverished, imposed, slippery, fickle, and almost wholly inconsistent.

And yet, there was this to it: it must be that I possessed a certain aspect, a certain meaning, a certain value for others, not only by reason of my physical features beyond the range of sight and fancy, but also on account of so many other things, to which, up to then, I had not given so much as a thought.

To think of this was to feel a fierce impulse to rebellion.

II

Discoveries

MY NAME, take it: ugly to the point of cruelty. *Moscarda*. *Mosca,* the housefly, and the shrill, annoying taunt of its tiresome buzz. The spirit that was I possessed no name whatsoever of its own; it possessed a whole world of its own that lay within; and I did not at every turn stamp with this, my name, to which in truth I gave no thought, all the things that I beheld within me and about me. All very good; but for others, I was not that nameless world which I carried around inside me, quite whole, undivided and yet varied. I was rather, on the outside, in their world, *one*—detached—who was called Moscarda, a tiny and determined aspect of reality that was not mine, locked up as I was outside myself in the reality of others and called *Moscarda*.

I was talking with a friend; there was nothing out of the ordinary in our conversation; I could see him gesticulating, and his voice and gestures were the usual ones, while he, as he stood there waiting to hear what I had to say, recognized mine as those he had known of old. There was nothing out of the ordinary, no, so long as I did not pause to reflect that the tone of my friend's voice for me was not at all the tone of voice that he knew, for the reason that he did not know at all the tone of that voice which was his; and his appearance, too, was as I saw it, that is, the one that I conferred upon him, looking at him from without, while he, as he spoke, assuredly did not have in his mind's eye any picture of himself, not even the one that he attributed to himself, and which he recognized upon glancing into a mirror.

Good heavens, and what was going to become of me, then? Was the same thing true of my voice, of my appearance? I was no longer an indistinct "I," who stood speaking to and looking at others, but one whom others in their turn looked at, outside themselves, and who possessed a tone of voice and an appearance that I did not recognize in myself. I was to my friend what he was to me, an impenetrable body which stood there in front of him, and which he depicted for himself with features that were well known to him, features which to me signified nothing; so true was this that I did not give them the slightest thought as I went on talking, nor could I see myself or know what manner of man I was; whereas for him they were everything, inasmuch as they depicted me as I was for him, one among many: *Moscarda*. Was it possible? And *Moscarda* was everything which that one said and did in that world to me unknown; *Moscarda* was also my shadow; *Moscarda*, if they saw him eating; *Moscarda*, if they saw him smoking; *Moscarda*, if he went for a walk; *Moscarda*, if he blew his nose.

I did not know it, I did not give it a thought, but in my appearance, that is to say, the one that they attributed to me, in my every word, which was uttered for them in a voice that I could never know,

in my every act, which was interpreted by each in
his own way, my name and my body to others were
always implicitly involved. The only thing is that,
by this time, however stupid and hateful a thing it
may have seemed to me, to be thus labeled forever,
without the possibility ever of giving myself another name, as many other names as I liked, as
might from time to time better accord with the
varying import of my deeds and feelings—notwithstanding all this, I repeat, I had by this time become
accustomed to bearing about with me from infancy
the name that I had, and was unable to bring myself
to make any great to-do about the matter, as I reflected that, after all, I was not that name, a name
which might be for others a none too pretty way
of distinguishing me, but which might have been a
good deal uglier than it was. Was there not, I should
like to know, a Sardinian at Richieri by the name
of Porcu?[1] There was.

"Signor Porcu—"

And he did not by any means respond with a
grunt.

"Here I am, at your service—"

Neat and courteous, he would respond with a
smile; until one was almost ashamed of having to
call him by a name like that.

But let us leave now the matter of name, and leave
likewise the matter of physical features, although I
now felt—now that, in front of the mirror, I had
had borne in upon me so sternly the essential impossibility of attributing to myself a likeness that was

---

[1] I.e., *pig.* (Translator.)

different from the one with which I was accustomed
to picture myself—I now felt that even those features were foreign to my will and spitefully opposed
to any desire that might arise in me of possessing
different ones, features that should not be these,
that is, hair like this, of this shade, eyes like these,
greenish, and this nose, and this mouth; and so, I
say, let us leave the matter of features likewise,
since, when all was said, I had to admit that they
might have been downright monstrous, in which
case, there would have been nothing to do but keep
them and resign myself to them, if I wished to go
on living; but they were not monstrous, and that
was that; I could, after all, bring myself to be quite
content with them.

But what about conditioning circumstances? I
mean, those conditions affecting me that did not
depend upon me. The determining conditions outside me, beyond any will of my own? Conditions of
birth and family? I myself had never confronted
them squarely, by way of evaluating them as others
were in a position to do, each in his own way, understand, with his own individual pair of scales, and
with the balancing weights of envy, hatred, contempt, or what not. I had believed myself up to then
to be a man in life. A man, that was it, and that was
enough. In life. Just as if I had made myself
whole. Whereas, it was not I who had fashioned
that body, who had given myself that name; I had
been brought into life by others without my will;
and similarly, through no will of my own, so many
things—above, within and round about—had come

to me from others; so many things had been done for me, given to me by others, things of which, as a matter of fact, I had never thought, of which I had formed no image like that weird, inimical one with which they came trooping over me now.

My family history! My family's history in the province. I had never given it a thought; yet that history, for others, was in me; I was an individual, the last of that family; I bore the mark of it in me, in my body, and who could say in how many habitual thoughts and actions, on which I never had reflected, but which it was obvious that others clearly recognized in me, in my manner of walking, of smiling, of exchanging a greeting. I believed myself a man in life, any man whatever, who went on like this, living an idle life from day to day, but one filled with curious, vagrant thoughts; but no, but no; I could be to myself any individual whatever, but not to others; for others, I possessed so many summarily distinguishing characteristics which I had never attributed to or manufactured for myself, and with which I had never concerned myself; that very ability of mine to believe myself any man, which is to say, that slothfulness which I looked upon as being my own, was to others no more mine than anything else; it was something that had been handed down to me by my father, that had to do with his wealth; and a terrible slothfulness it was, because my father—

Ah, what a discovery! My father— My father's life—

III

Roots

I COULD see him. Tall, heavy-set, bald. And in his limpid, almost glassy, pale-blue eyes, there shone for me the smile I knew so well, a strangely tender smile, with a hint of compassion in it, a trace of derision as well, but affectionate, as if at bottom he were glad that I was the sort of son to evoke his derisiveness; he all but regarded me, it seemed, as a freakish indulgence which he with impunity could afford to permit himself.

But now, as I looked back on it, that smile amid the thick wirey-rooted red beard that paled his cheeks, that smile beneath the heavy mustaches, a trifle yellowish in the middle—that smile was a lurking betrayal, a sort of mute and frigid grin, a thing which I had never noticed before. And that tenderness toward me which shone in his eyes, above that lurking grin, now impressed me as terribly malicious, so many things did it all at once reveal to me, things that sent shivers running up and down my spine. Yet the stare of those glassy eyes held me, held me fascinated, in such a manner as to prevent my thinking of those things which, when all was said, went to make up his tenderness toward me, but which to me were simply horrible.

"But supposing that you were and still are a dunce—yes, a poor, simple-minded scatterbrain who flies from one thought to another without ever halting one of them by way of bringing yourself to a halt; never does an idea pop into your head that you do not at once start circling all around it, and you continue gazing at it until you drop off to sleep; and the next day, when you open your eyes and behold it there in front of you still, you are no longer able to explain how it could ever have come into your head, assuming that yesterday's air and sun were the same as today's—I simply had to feel kindly toward you, you see; it was my duty. My hands? What are you staring at? Ah, these red hairs here, even on the back of my fingers? My rings—too many of them? And that big pin in my cravat, and the gold watch-chain as well— Too much gold? Why do you look at me like that?"

I perceived my uneasiness becoming strangely and with an effort diverted by those eyes, by all that show of gold, to come to rest upon a certain network of tiny and transparent bluish veins that crept laboriously up and up, over that pale forehead, over that shiny pate, circled by reddish hair, red like my own—that is, mine was like his—and how could it be mine, then, when it so obviously came to me from him? And that shiny pate, lo, little by little vanished from my sight, as if swallowed up in thin air.

My father!

Swallowed up in the void that was now, a terrified silence, heavy with all the insensate shapes which, in their inertia, their muteness and their impenetrability, are present to the human spirit. It was an instant, but it was eternity. I was conscious within of all the terror that comes from blind necessities, from things that cannot change: the prison of time; being born now, and not before or after; the name and body that is given one; the chain of causality; the seed which that man cast, my father without having willed it; my coming into the world, from that seed, that man's involuntary fruit, attached to that branch, sent up by those roots.

IV

The Seed

I SAW then my father for the first time, as I had never seen him before, externalized in his own life, but not as he had been to himself, not as he had felt himself to be, which was something I could never know; but rather, as a being that was wholly strange to me, in that reality which, as I now beheld him, I might suppose that others had imposed upon him.

The thing, I fancy, quite likely happens to all sons. It is to be noted that there is something mortifying for us and all but obscene where our fathers are concerned. It is to be noted, I am saying, that others do not attribute and cannot attribute to this father of ours the reality that we are in the habit of attributing to him. The discovery of how he lives a man's life outside of us, in his own right, in his relations with others, when these others, speaking to him or leading him on to speak with laughing glances round about him, forget for a moment that we are present. and so afford us a glimpse of the man they know in him, the man that he is for them. Another being. And how is that? We cannot know. Our father suddenly makes a sign, with his hand or with his eyes, that we are there. And that little, furtive sign, mark you, hollows out in us an inner abyss. He who was so very near to us, see how far away he has leaped, to be viewed there vaguely, like a stranger. And we feel as if our life had been wholly torn asunder, save for a point at which it remains yet attached to that man. And that point is a shameful one. Our birth, our detachment, our cutting off from him, is a common enough case, was possibly foreseen, and yet was an involuntary thing in the life of that stranger, the indication of a deed, fruit of an act, something in short that actually causes us shame, arousing in us scorn and almost hatred. And if it is not properly speaking hatred, there is a certain sharp contempt that we are now conscious of in our father's eyes also, which at this second happen to meet our own. We to him, as we stand upright on our feet here, with a pair of hostile eyes, are something that he did not expect from the satisfaction of a momentary need or pleasure, a seed that he unknowingly cast, a seed standing upright now on two feet, with a pair of popping snail's eyes that stealthily survey him and judge him and prevent him now from being wholly what he would like to be, free, *another man* even with respect to us.

V

Translation of a Title

I HAD never, up to now, detached myself like this from
my father. I had always thought of him, remembered him, as a father, for what he had meant to me,
which was, to tell the truth, exceedingly little, seeing that my mother had died very young and I had
been placed in a boarding school at a distance from
Richieri, then in a second and then in a third, where
I had remained until I was eighteen, after which I
went to the university and there spent six years
changing from one course to another without drawing any profit from any of them; this led to my being
called back to Richieri, where I was promptly married off, whether as a reward or a punishment, I
cannot say. Two years later, my father died, without leaving me any more lively memory of him, of
his affection for me, than that tender smile of his,
which was—as I have said—a mixture of pity and
derision.

As for what he had been to himself? He died
then, my father, altogether. As for what he had
been to others— And how little to me! It was
undoubtedly from others, from the reality which
they had imposed upon him, and which he suspected, that he had got that smile for me—I now
understood it all, understood the why of it all, and
it was horrible.

"What is your father?" my schoolmates so many times had asked me.

"A banker," I would reply. For the reason that, *to me,* my father *was* a banker.

Supposing that your own father were a hangman; how would that title be translated in your family to accord with the love you have for him and which he has for you? Oh, he is so very, very good to you; how well I know it; there is no need for you to tell me; I can picture perfectly the love of such a father for his small son, the tremulous delicacy of those big hands as they button up the little white nightshirt about his son's neck. And to think how ferocious those hands will be, at dawn tomorrow, upon the scaffold. In the same way, I am perfectly able to imagine a banker, going on from his ten to his twenty and his twenty to his forty per cent, while all the time, about the countryside, his reputation as a usurer is growing along with the distrust he inspires in others, a reputation that tomorrow will weigh like a burden of shame upon his young son, who for the moment is unconscious of it all, and who is amusing himself by playing hide-and-seek with out of the way thoughts, poor little freakish indulgence, who of a truth deserved—and it is I who am telling you—that tender smile which was made up half of pity and half of derision.

VI

A Good Lad But Wild

MY EYES horror-filled at this discovery, but with the horror veiled by a melancholy self-abasement which yet shaped my lips into a hollow smile, as the result of a suspicion that no one would be able to bring himself to believe or admit that any such emotions were mine, I thereupon betook myself to my wife, Dida.

She was standing—I remember—in a light-flooded room, clad in white and wholly wrapped in a glow of sun. being engaged in laying away in the big, white and gilt lacquered clothespress her new spring garments. In the bitterness of my secret shame, I made an effort to summon up a voice that would not appear too strange:

"I say, Dida, do you happen to know what my profession is?"

Dida, with a clothes-rack in her hand, from which hung a gown of the shade known as isabel, turned to look at me at first as if she did not recognize me. She was stunned.

"Your profession?" she repeated.

And I had to savor once again all the bitterness of my shame, by taking down as from a rent in my very soul the question that dangled there.

"Come," I said, "what do I do?"

Dida thereupon stood looking at me in astonish-

ment for a second, and then burst into a loud laugh:
"Why, what are you talking about, Gengè?"

That burst of laughter instantly shattered my
horror, routed the incubus of blind necessity,
against which my spirit, in its deep-going search,
had shiveringly bumped a short while before.

Ah, so that was it—a usurer to others, a
stupid fellow here at home, to Dida, my wife. I
was Gengè, an individual here and now, in my wife's
mind and eyes; and who could say how many other
Gengè's I was outside the house, in the minds or
merely in the eyes of the good people of Richieri?
It was not a matter that concerned my spirit, which
within me, in its pristine intimacy, felt free and
immune from the consideration of what had come
to me, what had been done to me, or what had been
attributed to me by others, and especially with regard to the question of money and my father's
profession. No? What did it concern, then? If I
was unable to recognize as my own that despicable
reality which others had imposed upon me, I still
had to admit, alas, that, even had I conferred one
upon myself, for myself, this would not have been
any truer *as reality* than that which others attributed to me, a reality that identified me with this
body which, here in the presence of my wife, I could
not feel was any more mine than the rest, especially
since *her* Gengè had appropriated it, that same
Gengè who just now had made another silly remark,
over which she had laughed so heartily. So, he
wanted to know his profession, did he? Just as if
he did not know it!

"A freakish indulgence," I said, almost to myself, detaching my voice from a silence that impressed me as being beyond life, for the reason that
I was a shade, here in front of my wife, and no
longer knew whence it was that I—I as I—ad-
dressed her.

"What are you talking about?" she repeated, out
of the assured solidity of her own life, and with
that isabel-hued gown over her arm.

And as I did not reply, she came toward me, took
me by the arms and breathed upon my eyelids, as if
to obliterate a glance that was no longer her
Gengè's, since she knew that it was Gengè's duty
as well as her own to pretend not to know how the
name of my father's profession was commonly
translated about the countryside.

But was not I even worse than my father? Ah!
My father at least had *worked*— But I? What
did I do? A good lad but wild. The good lad, who
talked of alien (even bizarre) things: of the discovery that the right side of my nose hung lower
than the left, or of the other face of the moon; and
meanwhile, what was known as my father's bank,
thanks to the management of my two faithful
friends. Firbo and Quantorzo, continued to *work,*
to prosper. There were minor shareholders in the
bank, and in addition, my two faithful friends
were what is known as co-partners; and everything
was going full sail ahead, without my burden-
ing myself with it in the least, thanks to the
good-will of my business associates, of Quantorzo,
who was like a son, and of Firbo, who was like a

brother, all of whom knew that it would have been useless to talk business to me, and that all that was necessary was to give me from time to time such information as was necessary to obtain my signature; I signed, and that was all there was to it. Not all; for from time to time, some one would come to ask me to go with him to see Firbo or Quantorzo with a word of recommendation; and what did I do then but discover upon his chin a dimple that divided it into two not wholly equal parts, one of which stood out a little more than the other.

How does it come that they had not knocked me in the head and had done with it long ago? Ah, my good people, there was a reason why they did not knock me in the head. Just as I up to then had never been sufficiently self-detached for a sight of myself, but went on living like a blind man under those conditions in which I had been placed, without pausing to consider what they were, for the reason that, having been born and brought up in them, they appeared to me natural, so it was equally natural to others that I should be as I was; they knew me like that; they would not have been able to think of me as being any different; and all might now look upon me without hatred, and even smile at this "good lad but wild."

All?

I was all of a sudden conscious of two pairs of eyes, driven into my soul like four poisoned daggers, the eyes of Marco di Dio and his wife, Diamante, whom I met every day in the street, upon my way home.

VII

Necessary Parenthesis, One for All

MARCO DI DIA and his wife, Diamante, had the fortune to be (if I rightly recall) my first victims. I mean, the first marked out for the experimental destruction of a Moscarda.

But what right have I to speak of them? What right have I here to attribute voice and appearance to others outside me? What do I know of them? How can I speak of them? I see them from without, and naturally as they are for me, that is, under a form in which they surely would not recognize themselves. And am I not then doing to others the same wrong of which I so complain?

Yes, certainly; but there is to be taken into account that little difference in fixations of which I have previously had something to say, the manner in which each one wills himself, building himself up so and so, as he really sees himself and sincerely believes himself to be, not only for himself but for all others as well. A presumption for which one has to pay the price, in one way or another.

You, I know, are not yet ready to give in.

"What about facts?" you exclaim. "Good heavens, is there no such thing as facts, the data of facts?"

"Yes, there is such a thing."

To be born is a fact. To be born at one time in-

stead of another, as I have already told you; and of
this or that father; in this or that station of life; in
Lapland or in Central Africa; handsome or ugly;
with or without a hunch on one's back: *facts.* And
even if you lose an eye, that is a fact; you may even
lose both eyes, and if you are a painter, that is the
most disagreeable fact that could come within your
experience.

Time, space: necessities. Fate, luck: accidents.
Life's traps, all of them. You will to be. There is
that. But in the abstract, there is no such thing.
Being must be snared in form, and for a time come
to an end in it, here or there, in this way or that.
Everything, so long as it endures, bears with it the
penalty of its own form, the pain of being the way
it is and of not being able any longer to be something other. That misshapen fellow there takes on
the appearance of a jest, the doubtful object of a
playful sympathy, for a minute only and no more;
and then, straight up, sharply, nimbly up—why,
yes, that is the way it is throughout this one and
only life of ours; and there is nothing to do but
resign one's self to spending the whole and all of it
like this.

The same thing is true of actions as of forms.
When an act is finished, it is what it is; it can no
longer change. Moreover, when one has acted, even
without his feeling and finding himself in the com-
pleted act, what he has done remains; it is like a
prison for him. Supposing that you have taken a
wife, or, what substantially is more to the point,
supposing that you have committed a robbery and

have been caught, or supposing that you have committed manslaughter; in each and any of these cases the consequences of your act envelop you, spiral-like, as with tentacles; and there is a weight upon you, above, around you, like a heavy-laden and unbreathable atmosphere—the responsibility for those actions, and for their consequences, which you have neither willed nor foreseen, but which none the less are thrust upon you. And how shall you ever be able to free yourself from them?

Very good. But what does it all mean? That actions like forms determine my and your reality? But how? Why? That they are a prison, no one can deny. But even if this is as far as you care to go in your assertions, see to it that you do not contradict me, when I state and maintain, as I hereby do, that they are not only a prison, but the most unjust sort of one that could be imagined.

I should think, good Lord, that I had proved it by now! I know Tizio. In accordance with the knowledge that I have of him, I attribute to him a reality: for me. But you also know Tizio, and the one that you know is not the one I know, for the reason that each of us knows him after his own fashion and, after his own fashion still, confers upon him a reality. Even for himself, then, Tizio has as many realities as there are individuals among us who know him; he knows himself in one fashion with me and in another fashion with you, and so on, with a third, a fourth, indefinitely. Which is equivalent to saying that Tizio is really one individual with me, another with you, another still with a third person,

yet another with a fourth, etc., while he himself—
he himself especially—all the while preserves the
illusion that he is one to all. The unfortunate thing,
or the amusing thing if you choose, is this. We go
through with an act. We believe in all good faith
that we have put ourselves wholly into that act.
We soon perceive, however, that it is not so, that
the act on the contrary is always and solely that of
one of the many persons that we are or may be capable of being when, unfortunately and unexpectedly,
we find ourselves strung up on a certain peg; we
perceive, I mean to say, that the whole of ourselves was not in that act, and that it would, accordingly, be a terrible injustice to judge us by that act
alone, to keep us strung up on that peg, as in a
pillory, for the whole of our existence, as if that
existence were wholly summed up in this one act.

"But I am also this one, and that one, and the
other one!" we start shouting.

So many, yes, indeed, so very many, so many
who remained quite outside the act of that one, and
who had nothing or very little to do with it. What
is more, that one himself, that is to say, that
momentary reality which is thrust upon us and
which, at a given moment, committed the act, very
often disappears altogether shortly afterward; as
an evidence of this, the memory of the act remains
in us, if it remains at all, as an inexplicable and
anguish-ridden dream. Another, ten others, all the
others that we are capable of being, rise up in us,
one by one, to ask how we ever could have done

a thing like that, and we are at a loss for an explanation.

Past realities.

If the facts of the case are not too grave, we term these past realities mistakes. This does very well; for the reason that every reality is a mistake. The very mistake that leads me to tell you, you have another one ahead of you.

"You are mistaken!"

We are very superficial, you and I. We do not make our way inside the jest, which is deeper, more deeply rooted than you think, my friends. It lies in this, that the being necessarily acts through forms, which are the appearances that it creates for itself, and to which we assign the value of reality. A value, naturally, that changes in accordance with the form and act in which the being becomes visible to us. It of necessity seems that others must have made a mistake, that an attributed form, an attributed act is not this and thus; but if, a little later, we shift our point of view, we inevitably become aware that we similarly have been mistaken, and that it is not this and is not thus; until in the end, we are constrained to recognize the fact that there will never be a this or a thus that is in any way stable or secure, but that, now in one manner, now in another, all at a certain point appear to be mistaken, or all appear to be right, which is the same thing. For reality is not a thing conferred upon us or which exists; it is something that we have to manufacture ourselves, if we will to be; and it will never be one

for all, one forever, but continuous and subject to
infinite mutations. The faculty of deluding one's
self that today's reality is the only true one, if on
the one hand it affords us a support, on the other
hand hurls us into a bottomless void, for the reason
that today's reality is destined to discover itself an
illusion tomorrow. And life knows no conclusion.
It cannot know any. If tomorrow there were to be
a conclusion, all would be over.

VIII

Come Down a Bit

ARE you thinking that I have taken you up too high?
Ah, well, come down a bit. The ball is elastic; but it
must touch earth, if it is to bounce. Suppose that
we touch earth, and let it bounce back into our
hands.

What are those facts that you are trying to tell
me about? The fact that I was born in such and
such a year, in such and such a month, on such and
such a day, in the worthy city of Richieri, in a house
in such and such a street, at such and such a number,
the son of Signor So-and-So of the So-and-So's and
of Signora So-and-So of the So-and-So's; that I was
baptized in Mother Church when I was six days old,
sent to school at the age of six, married at twenty-
three; and that I am one meter seventy in height, of
a reddish skin, etc., etc. That is my description.
Factual data, you say. And would you go on to deduce from it the reality that is mine? Do you fancy
that those data, which in themselves mean nothing,
hold an equal meaning and value for all? And
even if they succeeded in conveying a complete and
accurate picture of me, where would they picture me
as being? In what reality? In yours, which is not
that of another; and the same of another, and
another. Is there by any chance a sole reality, one
for all? Have we not already seen that there is

not even one for each of us, since our own inner reality is constantly changing! Well, then?

Look, here we are, back to earth—earth. How many of you are there, five? Come along with me.

This is the house in which I was born, in such and such a year, such and such a month, on such and such a day. Very good. From the fact that, topographically, by reason of its height and breadth and the number of windows here in front, this house is the same to all; from the fact that I, for all five of you, was born here, in such a year, such a month, on such and such a day, reddish of skin and a meter seventy in height; from all this do you think it follows that all five of you confer the same reality upon this house and upon me? To you, who live in a hovel, this house seems a beautiful palace; to you, who are possessed of a certain artistic taste, it seems a very vulgar sort of house indeed; you, who do not like to go down the street in which it stands, because it brings to mind an unpleasant episode in your life—you give it a surly glance; and you, on the other hand, survey it with a loving eye, for the reason—as I know—that your poor dear mother used to live directly across the street, she who was my own mother's good friend.

And I, who was born here? Good Lord! When, for all five of you, here in this house which is one and five, in such and such a year, such and such a month, on such and such a day, I was born a perfect imbecile, do you fancy that it was the same imbecile for all of you? For one, I may be an imbecile because I keep Quantorzo as director of the bank and Firbo for my legal adviser, which is the very reason why another holds me to be a most sagacious chap; this other rather sees a glaring evidence of my imbecility in the fact that I take my wife's bitch out walking every day, and so on. Five imbeciles, one in five. Five imbeciles here in front of you, as you behold them from without, in me, who am one and five like the house, all with this name of Moscarda, nothing in itself, not even a unit, since it serves to distinguish five imbeciles who, the moment someone sings out *Moscarda,* turn around, one and all of them, at one and the same time; but each one with that aspect which you attribute to him, five aspects; if he laughs, five smiles; and so on.

Is not every act that I perform, for you, the act of one of these five? And how can that act be the same, then, if the five are different? Each one of you will proceed to interpret it, to confer upon it a meaning and a value, in accordance with that reality which he has conferred upon me. One of you will say, "Moscarda did this," and another will reply, "What do you mean, he did that? It was something else entirely that he did!" And a third will say, "He did very well indeed, as I see it. He did just what he ought to have done!" "What he ought to have done! I like that! What he did was very bad. Now, what he ought to have done—" And the fifth: "What he ought to have done? What should you say if I told you, he did nothing at all!"

And you will be quite capable of coming to blows over what Moscarda did or did not do, over what he ought or ought not to have done, without being willing to understand that the Moscarda one knows is not the Moscarda of another; you believe that you are speaking of a single Moscarda, who is, you insist, one individual and no more, the one who stands in front of you in such and such a manner, whom you see, whom you touch; whereas you are really speaking of five Moscardas, for the reason that each of the other four similarly has one in front of him, who is one individual and no more, standing in such and such a manner, whom he sees and whom he touches; there are even six of you, if poor Moscarda sees and touches one on his own account; one and none, alas, the one that he sees and touches, since the other five see and touch him differently.

IX

Close the Parenthesis

NEVERTHELESS, have no fear, I shall strive to grant
you that reality which you believe you have; which
is equivalent to saying, I shall endeavor to will you
in me as you will yourselves. But it is not possible,
as you by this time well know, seeing that, however
hard I may strive to picture you after your own
manner, it will always be a "your manner" for me
alone, not a "your manner" for you and for others.

But excuse me; if for you I possess no reality
beyond that which you give me, if I am ready to
recognize and admit the fact that it is no less true
than the one I might be able to give myself, that it
is, even for you, the only true one (and Heaven
only knows what sort of a reality it is you are giving me!), have you any reason then to complain
of the one that I am about to give you, being
desirous in all good will of picturing you in so far
as possible after your own manner?

I do not presume that you are as I picture you.
No more are you, as I have already asserted, that
one whom you picture to yourselves, but rather any
number of beings at one and the same time, in accordance with all the possibilities of being that are
yours, and depending upon accidents, relations and
circumstances. Moreover, what harm am I doing
you? It is you who are harming me, by assuming

that I do not have, could not have, any other reality beyond the one that you give me—a reality, believe me, that is yours alone, an idea of your own, which you have made for yourselves of me, a possibility of being that you are conscious of, as it looks to you, the possibility of which you recognize in yourself; but as to what I am capable of being to myself, you not only can know nothing about that, but neither can I.

X

A Couple of Calls

I AM very glad that, just at this minute, as you are
engaged in reading this little book of mine with the
same somewhat bantering smile that from the first
has accompanied your reading, you should unexpectedly have received a couple of calls, one after
the other, by way of proving how silly that smile
of yours is.

You are still—I can see—disconcerted, irritated,
mortified over the extremely sorry figure you cut
with your old friend, by sending him away shortly
after the new one came in, with some shabby excuse
or other, simply because you could not any longer
endure seeing him there, because you could not
endure the sound of his voice and laugh in the
presence of the other. But what does it mean, your
sending him away like that, when, only a short
while before the other arrived, you were taking
so much pleasure in his merriment and his
conversation?

Sent him away. Whom? Your friend? And do
you seriously believe that it was he whom you sent
away.

Reflect a moment. There was nothing about your
old friend, in himself, to justify your sending him
away when the new one came. The two of them,
as a matter of fact, were not acquainted with each

116

other; it was you who introduced them; and they might have gone on and had a pleasant little chat for a half-hour or so, in your parlor, with no embarrassment to either of them. It was you who felt the embarrassment, and your embarrassment grew until it became unendurable, as you saw the two of them little by little drawing nearer to each other, and you perceived that they were getting on very well together. Why was this? Why it was because you—you (won't you understand?)—upon the arrival of your new friend, suddenly discovered that you were two separate persons, each of them different from the other; and as a result, not being able to endure it any longer, you simply had to send one of them away at a certain point. Not your old friend, no; it was yourself that you sent away, the self that you are to your old friend, for the reason that you felt that self to be altogether different from the one that you are, or would like to be, to your new friend.

They were by no means an incompatible pair, although they were two strangers; the attitude of one to the other was extremely courteous, and it may be that they were meant to get on marvelously well; but there were the two *you's* which you had, of a sudden, discovered in yourself, and you could not permit the affairs of one to be mingled with those of the other, inasmuch as the two of them had, in reality, nothing in common. Nothing, absolutely nothing, seeing that you for your old friend had one reality and another for the new one, the two being so diverse in character that you yourself could not help being aware of it; you knew that, upon your turning to one, the other would sit there looking at you in amazement; he would, perhaps, not be able to recognize you; he would exclaim to himself, "But how is this? Can it be that this is the person I know?" And in the insupportable embarrassment of finding yourself thus two persons, simultaneously, you began casting about for a shabby excuse for getting rid, not of one of them, but of one of the two of them that you were compelled at one and the same time to be.

Come, come, go back to reading my little book now, and do not smile over it any more, as you have been doing.

I would have you know, however, that if the experience you have just gone through has given you any slight displeasure, that is as nothing at all, old fellow, since you are not only two, but who can say how many, without knowing it, and all the time believing yourself one.

Let us be getting on.

BOOK FOURTH

I

What Marco di Dio and His Wife, Diamante, Were to Me

I say "were," but it may be that they are still living. Where? Here still, perhaps, so that it might be possible for me to see them tomorrow. But here, where? I no longer possess a world of my own; I am not in a position to know anything of them, wherever they may feign to be. I shall know for a certainty that they are going down the street, if tomorrow I encounter them in the street.

"You are Marco di Dio?" I shall ask him.

"Yes," he will reply, "Marco di Dio."

"And you are walking down this street?"

"Yes, down this street."

"And this is your wife, Diamante?"

"Yes, my wife, Diamante."

"And this street is named so-and-so?"

"So-and-so. And there are so many houses, so many cross-streets, so many lamp-posts, etc., etc."

Like in an Orlendorf's grammar.

Very well, this will satisfy me then, as it satisfies you now, so far as establishing the reality of Marco di Dio and his wife, Diamante, is concerned, and that of the street in which I may still encounter them as I encountered them in the past. When? Oh, not many years back. What an admirable precision is that of time and space! The street, five

years back. Eternity has yawned for me, not only
in the course of those five years, but from one minute to another. And the world in which I then lived
impresses me as being farther away than the
farthest star of heaven.

Marco di Dio and his wife, Diamante, as I beheld
them, were an unfortunate pair who, on the one
hand, as a result of their wretched condition, had
become persuaded that it was a futile thing to keep
on washing their faces every morning, but who, on
the other hand, undoubtedly were persuaded that it
was their duty to leave no stone unturned, not by
way of earning the mere daily pittance which sufficed to keep them from going hungry, but toward
becoming overnight millionaires—*mil-lion-aires,* as
he, spacing the word into syllables, put it, with a
scowl from his ferocious, wide-staring eyes. I
laughed then, and all laughed with me, at hearing
him talk like this. I am horrified now, to think that
I could have laughed like that, simply because, as it
happened, I had not yet been brought to doubt that
corroborating and highly providential thing which
is known as the regularity of experience; and so it
was that I could regard as a comical dream the idea
of becoming a millionaire overnight. But supposing
that this very fine thread, as it has before now been
shown to be, by which I mean the regularity of experience, had been broken off in me? Supposing
that, from repeating itself two or three times, that
same comical dream had, on the contrary, acquired
for me a certain *regularity?* Even I then would

have come to the point where I should have held it impossible to doubt that one really might become a millionaire from one day to the next. Those who hold to the blessed regularity of experience will not be able to imagine the things that may be real or true-seeming to one who lives beyond any rule, which is exactly what this man did.

He believed himself to be an inventor; and an inventor, my good people, wakes up one fine day, invents something, and there you are! He becomes a millionaire!

There were any number who remembered him as an uncouth fellow who had just come up from the country to Richieri.   They recalled how he had been taken into the studio of one of our best-known artists, now dead, and how, within a short time, he had learned to work in marble with considerable skill.   And then, one day, the sculptor decided to take him as a model for one of the figures in the group which he was at that time engaged upon, and which later, when exhibited in plaster at an art show, became famous under the title of *Satyr and Boy*. The artist had succeeded in harmlessly transferring to clay a fantastic vision, not a chaste one certainly but a very lovely one, one in which he himself could take delight and which won him the praise of others.

The crime was in the clay.

The sculptor did not suspect that there might spring up in his pupil a temptation to transfer in his turn that fantastic vision from the clay, where it

had been praiseworthily fixed for ever, to a momentary action that was no longer deserving of praise;
which was what happened as, oppressed by the sultriness of a summer afternoon, the pupil labored
away in the studio at rough-casting the group in
marble.   The real-life boy was not possessed of the
smiling docility that the fictitious one displayed in
the clay; he screamed for help, people came running in, and Marco di Dio was surprised in an act
which was that of the beast in him, a beast which,
in that sultry moment, had unexpectedly broken
loose.

Let us be just, now: a beast, yes; the filthiest sort
of beast, in that act; but in view of all his other acts,
honestly vouched for, did not Marco di Dio perhaps
come nearer to being that commendable youth
whom his master said he had always known his
helper to be?   I realize that, with this question, I am
offending your sense of morality.   You will, in
truth, answer me by saying that the fact that such
a temptation could spring up in Marco di Dio is an
evident sign that he was not the commendable
young man that his master said he was.   I would
merely call your attention as we go along to the
horde of similar temptations (and even baser ones)
to be found in the lives of the saints.   The saints
attributed them *to the power of the demons,* and
with God's aid were enabled to overcome them.
Just as those restraints which you habitually impose upon yourselves customarily keep such temptations from arising in you, preventing the robber or
the assassin from suddenly bursting forth.   The op-

pressive sultriness of a summer's afternoon has never sufficed to liquefy the crust of your habitual probity, or to kindle in you even for a moment the beast primeval. You may pass sentence.

But what if I, at this moment, start talking of Julius Caesar, whose imperial glory so fills you with admiration?

"Vulgar!" You will exclaim. "He was no longer Julius Caesar then. We admire him where Julius Caesar was truly *himself.*"

Splendid. Himself. But don't you see? If Julius Caesar was *himself* only where you admire him, when he was no longer there, where was he? Who was he? No one? Anyone? And who?"

We should have to ask Calpurnia, his wife, or Nicomedes, King of Bithynia.

Talk on and on; and by the time you are through, the further thought will have occurred to you: that Julius Caesar, the individual, did not exist. There existed, it is true, a Julius Caesar that we know from so large a part of his life, and this one undoubtedly possesses a value incomparably greater than the others; not, however, so far as reality is concerned, please believe me when I tell you that; for not any less real than this imperial Julius Caesar was that simpering, effeminate creature, all shaved and ungirdled and anything but faithful to his wife, Calpurnia; and the same might be said of the utterly shameless Nicomedes, King of Bithynia.

The unfortunate part, my good people, is as usual this, that every last one of them had to be called by the single name of Julius Caesar, and that in a single

body of masculine sex, they all had to live together
alongside a woman, who, wanting to be a woman
and not finding the way in that masculine body, had
to be one retrogressively, where and as she could,
shamelessly and unnaturally, on more than one
occasion.

The satyr in that poor devil of a Marco di Dio,
we have good reason to believe, broke out only once,
when tempted by the sculptor's figures. Surprised
in this act of a moment, he was condemned forever.
There was no one he could find who would show
him any consideration; and so, when he came out
of prison, he began casting about for the most
whimsical sort of plans that might make it possible
for him to get out of the disgrace and want into
which he had fallen; and with him, arm-in-arm,
went a woman, who one fine day had come to him,
none knew how nor from where. He had been saying, for ten years gone by now, that he was going
to England the coming week. But had those years
really gone by for him, after all? They had gone
by for those who had heard him say it. He was
always resolved upon setting out for England next
week. He even studied English; or at any rate, for
some years past, he had carried an English grammar
under his arm, open and turned down always at the
same page, so that those two open pages, from the
brushing of his arm and the grime of his coat sleeve,
had become by now thoroughly illegible, while the
following pages remained incredibly clean. But up
to the greasy spot, he knew his grammar; and from
time to time, as he went down the street, he would

turn without warning and put to his wife abruptly some question or other, as if he were trying out her promptness and preparedness:

"*Is Jane a happy child?*"

And his wife would reply, promptly and with all due gravity:

"*Yes, Jane is a happy child.*"

For the wife, too, was going to England with him, next week.

It was at once dismaying and a pity, the sight of this woman whom he had contrived to attract to himself, and whom he forced to live the life of a faithful dog in this comical dream world of his, the dream of becoming an overnight millionaire through some such invention as "*non-odorous cesspools for localities without water in the houses*"— You laugh at this? That is why they were so truculent in their gravity! I mean, because everybody laughed at them. They were downright ferocious about it; and their ferocity grew as the laughter about them waxed louder. They had now reached the point where, if anyone stopped to listen to their schemes without laughing, they, instead of being pleased by it, would dart him terrible sidelong looks, not so much of suspicion as of hatred. For the derision of others was by this time the very air in which their dream lived and breathed; take the derision away, and they ran the risk of suffocating.

All this goes to make it clear to me why it was my father had been their worst enemy. For the truth is, I was not the only one who afforded him an opportunity for that freakish indulgence of which I have spoken above. He took pleasure in helping along, with a bounty of which he never tired, smiling that peculiar smile of his, the stolid illusions of certain ones who, like Marco di Dio, would come to him to weep over their unhappiness at not having sufficient to carry out their plans, their dream—wealth!

"How much?" my father would ask.

Oh, a very little. For a very little was always enough to enable such as these to become rich, million-aires. And my father would give it.

"But how is that? You told me that you only needed a little—"

"That's true; but my calculations were not quite right. Now, if only—"

"How much?"

"Oh, a very little."

And my father gave and gave. But when a certain point was reached, he would decide that he had had enough; and it is easy to understand then that they were far from being grateful to him for not having cared to see the jest through, to their total disillusionment; they might now attribute to him, plausibly and remorselessly, the bankruptcy of their illusions. No one could have been more furious than such as these in seeking revenge, which they found by calling my father a usurer.

The most infuriated of all had been this Marco di Dio, who now, my father being dead, spilled upon me, and not without good reason, the whole of his fierce hatred. Not without good reason, since I too, almost without knowing it, was continuing to be his benefactor, by keeping him lodged in a certain hovel on my estate, for which neither Firbo nor Quantorzo had ever demanded any rent. And it was this very hovel which now provided me with the means of attempting upon him my first experiment.

II

It Was Thoroughgoing

THOROUGHGOING, for the reason that, by arousing in
me, little by little, as if it had been a sort of game,
the will to exhibit myself as different from one of
the hundred-thousand in whom I lived, it at the same
time altered in a hundred-thousand ways all my
other realities.

It was inevitable, if you think it over well, that
this game of mine should yield the fruit of madness.
Or, better, this horror: the consciousness of madness, as clear and fresh, good people, as fresh and
clear as an April morning, as shining and precise
as a mirror.

For in embarking upon this first experiment, I
was about to put from me my will, as gracefully as
if I had been taking a handkerchief out of my
pocket. I desired to go through with an act which
should not be my own, but the act of that shadow
of myself who was a living reality in another, a
reality so veracious and solid-seeming that I might
have taken off my hat to it, if by a cursed necessity
I had not had to meet and greet it in the flesh, not
in myself to be exact, but in my own body, which,
being no one in itself, could be and was mine in so
far as it represented me to myself, but which also
could be and was that shadow's, belonging to those
hundred-thousand shadows which represented me

130

as living and diverse, in a hundred-thousand ways
to a hundred-thousand others.

Was I not in all truth, setting out to play a dirty
trick upon Signor Vitangelo Moscarda? Yes, good
people, that is what it was! a dirty trick (you will
have to excuse all these winks on my part, but I
have need of winking, to wink like this, since, not
being aware just what impression I am making
upon you at this moment, I may be able thus to
obtain a hint), by making him go through with an
act that was wholly contrary to and inconsistent
with his being, an act which, by destroying at one
blow his logical reality, would thereby annihilate
him at once in the eyes of Marco di Dio, and who
could say how many others as well? I did not perceive, poor wretch! that the consequences of an act
like this could not be as I pictured them. I imagined
that, afterward, I would face one and all with the
question: "Do you see now, gentlemen, there's not
a word of truth in it—I am not the usurer that you
like to behold in me?" Whereas what was to happen
was, rather, this: all would exclaim in dismay: "Oh!
oh! did you hear the news? Moscarda, the usurer,
has gone mad!"

Because Moscarda, the usurer, could go mad; but
he could not, thus at a blow, destroy himself, by an
act contrary to and inconsistent with himself. The
usurer, Moscarda, was not a wraith to be played
with and mocked at; he was a gentleman to be
treated with all due respect, one meter seventy in
height, reddish of skin, like his dad before him, the
founder of a bank and— Ah, yes—with circumflex-

accent eyebrows, and that nose that sagged to the right, like the nose of my wife Dida's dear but stupid Gengè; a gentleman who, Lord preserve us, by going mad ran the risk of dragging along to the insane asylum with him all the other Moscardas that I was to others, and even, good Lord, that poor innocuous Gengè, my wife Dida's property; and finally, I must tell you, even myself, who had played the game all along with an airy smile.

I ran the risk—or rather, as you shall see, we ran the risk, every man of us—of the insane asylum that first time. And that was not enough; we had to risk our lives as well, in order that I in the end (one, none and a hundred-thousand) might find and resume the path of well-being.

But let us not get ahead of our story.

III

At the Notary's

I BETOOK myself first of all to the office of Stampa, the notary, in the Via del Crocefisso, No. 24. For the reason that (and these are most assuredly factual data), on the —— day of the year ————, in the reign of Victor Emmanuel III, by the grace of God and the will of the people King of Italy, in the worthy city of Richieri, in the Via del Crocefisso, at the official number 24, there was one Signor Cav. Elpidio Stampa who kept a notary's office.

"It is still there? At No. 24? So, you all know Notary Stampa?"

Ah, then, we can be quite sure that we are not mistaken. That Notary Stampa, then, whom you all know. Righto? But you cannot imagine what a state of mind I was in as I entered his office. How could you imagine it, please be so good as to tell me, when it seems to you still the most natural thing in the world to enter a notary's office for the purpose of recording any transaction, whatever it may be, and when you assure me that you all are acquainted with this same Notary Stampa. I am telling you that I went there, on this particular day, for the first experiment; and the short of the matter is, do you or do you not care to make this experiment with me, once and for all? What I mean is, do you feel like fathoming the terror-inspiring jest that lies

133

beneath the pacific natural-seemingness of daily
relations, those relations which impress you as altogether normal and ordinary, beneath the tranquil
appearance of the so-called reality of things? This,
in the name of Heaven, is the same jest that works
you up into a fury every five minutes or so, and
which causes you to exclaim to the friend at your
side, "I beg your pardon! But how does it come that
you don't see this? Are you blind?" And your
friend does not see it, but sees another thing, when
you all the while feel that he ought to be seeing
what you see, as you see it. He, on the contrary,
sees it as it appears to him; and for him, therefore,
the blind man is yourself.

This is the jest I am telling you of, as I already
had fathomed it.

I now entered that office burdened with all the
reflections and considerations over which I had for
so long been brooding; I could feel them, as it were,
sputtering inside me and making a great hubbub;
and I all the while was doing my best to preserve a
certain lucid fixity, a certain immobile frigidity.
You can understand, then, how it was that I came
to burst out laughing noisily, upon catching sight
of that poor little notary, Signor Stampa, with a
face that was all gravity and without the faintest
suspicion that I could be to myself any other being
than the one he saw before him, so sure was he that,
to me, he was the same individual who every day
beheld himself in the mirror, knotting his little
black cravat, with familiar objects all around him.
Do you get it, now? I simply had to wink at him,

too, by way of signifying roguishly, *"Look under-neath! Look underneath!"* And what's more, Heaven help me, I had to stick out my tongue, when he least expected it, and suddenly screw up my nose, all without any maliciousness and as a kind of game, by way of altering at one stroke that image of me which he believed to be the true one. But serious about it, eh? Nothing if not serious. I had to go through with the experiment.

"Well, Signor Notary, here I am. But if you don't mind my asking you, are you all the time sub-merged in a silence like this?"

He turned his head sharply and looked me over.

"Silence?" he said. "Where?"

It is true that, out in the Via del Crocefisso at that moment, there was an incessant coming and going of people and vehicles.

"Oh, not out in the street, to be sure. But there are all those papers, Signor Notary, behind the dusty panes of that case. Don't you hear some-thing?"

Half-perturbed and half-dumfounded, he turned on me another searching look; then, he listened:

"What is there to hear?"

"Why, that rasping sound! Ah, I beg your par-don, it is the claws of your canary there; I beg your pardon. They are sharp, those little claws, and when they rasp against the zinc of the cage—"

"Quite so, quite so. But what difference does it make?"

"Oh, none at all. But doesn't that zinc get on your nerves, Signor Notary?"

"The zinc? Who thinks of that? I don't notice it—"

"And yet, just think! the zinc of a cage beneath the slender little paws of a canary, in a notary's office— I'll wager, that canary of yours doesn't sing."

"No, sir, he doesn't sing."

From the looks the Signor Notary had begun to give me, I deemed it prudent to let the subject of the canary drop, in order not to endanger the success of the experiment; for at the beginning, and especially here, in the presence of the notary, it was important that no doubt should arise regarding my mental faculties. I accordingly went on to ask the Signor Notary if he knew a certain house, situated in such-and-such a street, at such-and-such a number, being the appurtenance of a certain Signor Vitangelo Moscarda, son of the late Francesco Antonio Moscarda—

"And isn't that you?"

"Precisely, I. That is—"

It was all too lovely, sitting in that notary's office, amid all those yellowing documents in those old dust-laden cases, to be speaking like this, as at a distance of centuries, of a certain house as being the appurtenance of a certain Vitangelo Moscarda— And it was all the lovelier by reason of the fact that I was there—even so—present and covenanting, in that notary's office; yet who could say what sort of office it was or where it was for the Signor Notary himself. What odor did he scent that was different from the one that met my nostrils? Or who could say what was the location and manner of being in the Signor Notary's world of that particular house, of which I had been speaking to him in a far-away voice; and I, and I, in the Signor Notary's world, how very curious, perhaps—

Ah, the pleasures of history, good people! Nothing is more restful than history. Everything in life is continually changing under our very eyes; there is nothing certain; and that restless desire to know how accidents shape themselves, to see how facts take on stability, facts that keep you so breathlessly agitated! Everything, on the other hand, is shaped and stabilized in history; however sad the accidents may be, however dolorous the vicissitudes, you there behold them put in order, or at least fixed, in from thirty to forty small pages of a book; here they are, never more to change, unless some perfidious critical mind comes along and is not content until he has bowled over our idealistic edifice, in which all the elements in succession were so nicely adjusted, leaving one with a tranquillizing feeling of wonderment at the manner in which every effect obediently followed its cause in perfectly logical fashion, while every event evolved accurately and consistently, with my Lord, the Duke of Nevers, who on such-and-such a day, in such-and-such a year, etc., etc.

In order not to spoil everything, I had to bring my mind back to the wavering, temorary, jumbled reality of the Signor Notary Stampa.

"Yes," I hastened to assure him, "it is I. It should be, Signor Notary. As for the house, I presume you will find nothing in the way to admitting that it is mine, like all the rest of the hereditary estate of the late Francesco Antonio Moscarda, my father. So far, so good. Likewise, Signor Notary, the fact that the house in question is not rented at the present time. Oh, I know, it's a small one— There must be five or six rooms, with a couple of low wings—I believe that's what you call them?— they're very nice, those wings— It's standing idle, then, Signor Notary, and I am in a position to dispose of it as I may see fit. Well, then, you—"

At this point, I leaned over and, in a low voice, with great gravity, confided to the Signor Notary the step I intended to take, and which here, for the present, I cannot relate.

"It is a matter between me and you, Signor Notary," I said to him; "it must remain a professional secret, so long as I deem it best. Are we agreed?"

It was agreed. But the Signor Notary called my attention to the fact that, in order to go through with this transaction, he would have to have certain data and documents which I should have to go to the bank to get from Quantorzo. I felt thwarted; however, I arose. As I did so, there sprang up in me an execrable impulse, to put a certain question to the notary: "Excuse me, but how do I walk? You might at least tell me how it looks to you!" I was holding myself in with difficulty; but I could not resist turning, as I opened the glass-paned door, to remark to him with a pitying smile: "Why, with my own stride, thanks!"

"What's that you say?" queried the astonished notary.

"Ah, nothing at all; I was merely observing that it is with my own stride I am going off. Did you know that I once heard a horse laugh? Yes, sir, I did, while the horse was walking. And now, you are going to go looking at a horse's mouth to see him laugh, and you will be coming to tell me that you did not see him laugh. But what do you mean, looking at his mouth! Horses don't laugh with their mouths, not by any means! Do you know what it is horses laugh with, Signor Notary? With their behinds. I assure you that a horse, when he is walking, laughs with his behind, from time to time— he surely does—either at certain things which he sees, or at things that run through his head. And so, if you want to see a horse laugh, look at his behind, and you can't go wrong!"

I know that this kind of talk on my part was wholly irrelevant. I know all that. What I have to do is to put myself back into the frame of mind in which I then was. When I saw people's eyes upon me, it seemed to me that I was submitting to a horrible tyranny, since all those eyes were attributing to me a self-likeness which was certainly not the one I knew, but another, one that I could neither know nor ward off. And it was then the temptation came to me not only to say but to do— to do—mad things, such as rolling over and over in the street, or bouncing up like a ball, now giving a wink, now sticking out my tongue, now making frightful grimaces— But instead, I went down the street as gravely and seriously as could be—yes, I—I went down the street. And the charming part of the matter is that you likewise, all of you, were going along as seriously as could be—

IV

Main Street

I HAD, then, to go to the bank for those papers that the notary needed concerning the house. Those papers were mine, there could be no doubt of that, inasmuch as the house was mine and I was in a position to dispose of it. But if you stop to think, I should never have been able to get those papers except by theft, or by snatching them with a mad violence from the hands of another who, in the eyes of all, was the legitimate owner; I mean, Signor Vitangelo Moscarda, the usurer. To me, this was clear enough, for I saw that usurer, Signor Vitangelo Moscarda, well from without; but in the sight of others, who beheld in me none other than that same usurer, I was on my way to the bank to rob myself of those papers, or else to snatch them madly from my own hands.

Was I to say, perhaps, that I was not I? Or that I was another? There was no way of reasoning out an act which, in the eyes of all, was deliberately intended to appear contrary to and inconsistent with myself.

I kept on walking, you will note, with perfect consciousness down the main street of madness, which was none other than Reality Street to me, and which had now opened up most dazzlingly before me, with all the likenesses of myself, validly mirrored and alive, stalking along beside me.

141

But it was precisely because I possessed this accurate-mirroring consciousness that I was mad. You, on the other hand, who go down this same street without caring to take any notice of it, you are the wise ones, and your wisdom grows as you raise your voices to shout at the one who walks beside you:

"I this one? I like that? You are blind! You are mad!"

V

Domineering

Theft, however, was not possible, at least not there
and then. I did not know where those papers were.
The lowest of Quantorzo's or of Firbo's sub-
ordinates had more to say in that bank than I did.
When I went there, upon the management's invitation, the employes did not so much as lift their
eyes from their ledgers; and if one of them did
happen to give me a glance, that glance showed
only too clearly that he did not consider me as of the
slightest importance. And yet, there they all were,
working away so zealously for me, in order to clench
more and more, with their assiduous toil, the unfortunate conception of myself that was prevalent
about the countryside, to the effect that I was a
usurer. And it did not so much as occur to any of
them that, in place of being pleased with and disposed to praise them for their zeal, I might be
offended by it.

Ah, what stiffness, weariness and squalor there
was in that bank! All those glass partitions that
ran in a row for the length of the three big rooms,
partitions of frosted glass, with five yellow wickets
in each one, the same yellow that was to be seen
on the cornices and the woodwork of the broad
plate-glass windows; here and there were ink-stains,
and here and there a strip of paper or two had been

143

pasted over a crack in the plate glass; the old terra-
cotta brick pavement, worn away in the center,
which ran the length of the three huge rooms; worn
away, likewise, in front of each wicket—a gloomy
corridor, that, with the glass of the partitions on
one side, in each room, and on the other the dusty
panes of the two broad windows; those strings of
figures along the walls, scrawled up with pen or
pencil, over the little ink-spattered tables, between
one window and another, beneath the peeling
frames of certain nameless old pictures, black with
soot and dusty and distended here and there; and a
smell of ancient mould everywhere, mingled with
the acrid odor of paper from the ledgers and with
the aridity exhaled by a furnace down below, on the
ground-level.   And the despairing melancholy of
those few old-fashioned chairs upon which no one
sat, over by the little tables; they had shoved them
to one side and left them there where they did not
belong, and for those poor useless chairs, it must
have been an insult and an affliction to be left like
that. How many times, upon coming into the place,
had I had it on the tip of my tongue to remark:
"But why those chairs? Why have they been sen-
tenced to stand over there, where no one makes use
of them?" I had, however, restrained myself, and
not merely because I had reflected in time that, in
such a place as this, any sympathy manifested for
chairs would have struck everyone with amazement
and would, not unlikely, have sounded like a bit of
cynicism; I had restrained myself, rather, because
I knew that I would only raise a laugh at my own

expense; my noticing such a thing would certainly have appeared whimsical to anyone who knew how little attention I paid to business matters.

On this day, as I came in, I found the employes all collected in the farthest of the three big rooms, and I could hear squirts of laughter from them now and then, as they listened to an altercation between Stefano Firbo and one Turolla, who served as a butt to all the others by reason of the manner in which he dressed. A long coat, poor Turolla was in the habit of observing, short as he was, would have made him look shorter still. And he was right. But the stubby, pompous little man, with his great, swaggering mustaches, was unaware of how ridiculous he looked in that little short coat, which afforded a glimpse of his sturdy behind. Bantered and humiliated by the loud laughter of his associates, he was very red in the face and on the verge of tears, as he raised a diminutive arm to Firbo.

"My God," he said, "how you talk!"

Firbo was towering over Turolla and shouting in the latter's face, shaking him furiously by that upraised arm of his:

"So, you think so, do you! What do you know about it? What do you know about it? You don't know the first thing about it!"

I learned that the row was over a certain individual who had requested a loan of the bank, after he had been introduced by Turolla, who stated that he knew him to be an excellent fellow, while Firbo maintained the contrary; and upon hearing this, I felt torn by an impulse to rebellion. Being ignorant of my hidden spiritual torment, none of them could understand the reason for this; and they nearly fainted when I suddenly stepped up and jerked two or three of them back.

"What about yourself?" I shouted at Firbo. "What do you know about it? What right have you to domineer over another like that?"

Firbo turned and stared at me in bewilderment; it was as if he could not believe his eyes.

"Are you mad?" he cried.

I do not know how it came about, but I thereupon hurled an insult in his face, one that froze them all:

"Yes, like that wife of yours, whom you ought to keep locked up in an insane asylum!"

He faced me, pale and convulsed:

"What's that you say? I ought to do what?"

I shrugged my shoulders. Wearied of the general discomfiture and, at the same time, suddenly deafened as it were by an inner consciousness of the inopportuneness of this interference on my part, I gave him a soft answer, by way of cutting the matter short:

"Why, yes, you know it very well."

I cannot tell you how it happened, but no sooner had I uttered these words than I seemed to turn to stone; and I was not able to hear what it was that Firbo shouted at me between his teeth, as he burst out of the room in a rage. I know that I was smiling as Quantorzo, who had taken a hand in the dispute, dragged me away with him into the little private office. I smiled to show that there was no necessity for any further violence, that all was over; and yet,

I felt clearly enough inside me that, at that moment, even while I was smiling, I would have been capable of killing some one, so irritated was I by Quantorzo's overwrought severity. Once in the private office, I looked about me; I was astonished that the strange numbness which had swooped down upon me so all of a sudden did not prevent an accurate and lucid perception of material things; so strong was this feeling that I all but had the temptation to laugh, and in the midst of Quantorzo's stern reprimand, I broke out with some childishly curious questions concerning this or that object in the room. And then, too, I somehow almost automatically thought of Stefano Firbo as a lad, and of how they had given him buttons down the back; if his hump was no longer visible, the whole upper part of his body was none the less stooped—a hump all over, that is what it was—above those long, birdlike legs of his; but he was a dandy, for all of that, a false-humped dandy, well turned out. As my thoughts ran along like this, it dawned upon me that what he ought to do was to make use of his out-of-the-ordinary intelligence in revenging himself upon all those who, as lads, had not like himself had buttons down the back.

I thought these things, I may tell you once again, as if another had been thinking in me, one who, all unforeseen by me, had become so strangely cold and distracted. It was not so much that he purposed at need to throw up that coldness as a defense; he was, rather, acting a part, behind which it behooved me to keep hidden yet the things which I was all the time discovering out of that frightful verity which already had been made clear to me.

"Why, yes," I thought, "that is the whole thing, this domineering. Each one wants to impose upon others that world he has within, as if it were an outward entity, as if all ought to see it after his fashion, it being impossible for others to exist there save as he sees them."

I had a glimpse once more of the stupid faces of all those employes:

"Ah, yes! Ah, yes! What sort of reality can that be which the majority of mankind succeed in setting up inside themselves? Wretched, slippery, uncertain. And the domineering ones, mark you, profit by it! Or better, they are under the illusion of being in a position to profit by it, by causing to be submissively accepted that meaning and that value which they attribute to themselves, to others, and to things, in order that all may see and hear, think and speak after their manner."

Vastly relieved, I arose from my seat and went over to the window; then I turned to Quantorzo who, interrupted in the middle of his lecture, now stood there glaring at me. I went on with the thought that was torturing me:

"Ah, yes! Ah, yes! They're deluding themselves!"

"Who's deluding himself?"

"Those that try to domineer! Signor Firbo, for example! They are deluding themselves, since the truth is, my dear fellow, all they succeed in imposing on another is words. Words, understand?

Words that each one hears and repeats to suit himself. But, we must not forget, they go to make up what is commonly known as public opinion! And woe to him who one fine day finds himself branded with one of those words that everybody goes about repeating. For example, *usurer!* For example, *madman!* There is one point, however, on which I wish you would give me a little enlightenment, and that is, how you can rest quietly when you reflect that there is someone who is doing his utmost to persuade others that you are as he sees you, endeavoring firmly to establish you in the estimation of others in accordance with his judgment of you, and to prevent others from seeing and judging you in any other manner?"

I barely had time to observe Quantorzo's stupefaction, when whom should I see before me again but Stefano Firbo? I could make out, at once, from the look in his eyes that he had become, in the course of a few moments, my enemy. With an equal suddenness, I thereupon became his enemy; I was his enemy because he would not understand that, however harsh my words may have been, the feeling which a short while before had welled up in me had not been directed at him personally. So true was this that I was now ready to beg his forgiveness for those words. I even, like a drunken man, went further, as he came storming up to me with menace in his face and bearing.

"I want you to give an accounting," he said, "for that remark you just made about my wife."

I dropped to my knees.

"Why, certainly!" I cried. "Look! Like this!"
And I touched the stones of the floor with my fore-head.

I was immediately horror-struck by this act, or rather, at the idea that he could believe with Quantorzo that it was to him I had knelt. I looked up at them with a laugh, and—bump, bump—twice more my head went down.

"You, not I—understand?—to your wife—understand?—ought to be doing this! And I, and he, and all the others, to all the so-called madmen—ought to be doing this!"

I leaped to my feet, all a-tremble. The two of them stood there staring me in the eyes, and there was terror in their gaze.

"What's he talking about?" one of them asked the other.

"New words!" I shouted. "Do you want to hear them? Then go—go there where you keep those people locked up; go, go and listen to them talk! You keep them locked up because it's more convenient for you!"

I seized Firbo by his coat collar and shook him, with a laugh:

"Do you understand, Stefano? Don't think that you are the only one I have it in for! You are offended. No, old man! What was it your wife was saying about you? That you are a libertine, a robber, a forger, an impostor, and that everything you say is lies! It's not true. No one could believe it. But before you shut her up, eh? we all stood about listening to her, and we were thoroughly scared. What I want to know is, why!"

Firbo barely gave me a glance, but turned to Quantorzo as if to seek the latter's advice. When he spoke, it was with a foolish dismay:

"Oh, well, if you want to know! It was simply because nobody *could* believe it!"

"Ah, no, old man!" I was still shouting. "Look me in the eyes!"

"What are you trying to say?"

"Look me in the eyes!" I repeated. "I'm not saying it's true! Stand still."

He forced himself to look at me, turning pale as he did so.

"Do you see it?" again I shouted, "Do you see it? You yourself! You have it, too, now; there is terror in your eyes!"

"That's because you're acting like a madman!" he screamed at me in his exasperation.

I burst out laughing, a long, long laugh, a laugh that I could not restrain, as I observed the fear and tumult that my laughter occasioned in the pair of them. I stopped suddenly, terrified in my turn by the eyes that were fixed on mine. What I had been saying and doing assuredly had no rhyme or reason for them. I strove to regain possession of myself.

"Let's cut it short," I said. "I came here today to request an accounting of you with respect to a certain Marco di Dio. I should like to know why it is that, for all these years, that fellow has gone on without paying any rent, while you have taken no steps whatever toward evicting him."

They were as stupefied as I could possibly have anticipated at this question. They stood looking at each other, as if each were seeking in the other's gaze for a support that would enable him to bolster up his impression of me, or rather, his impression of a stranger whom they, unexpectedly and unsuspectingly, had discovered in me.

"What in the world are you talking about?" Quantorzo asked.

"What's the matter? Can't you get your wits together? Marco di Dio. Does he or does he not pay his rent?"

They continued to look at each other with gaping mouths. I burst out laughing again; and then, without warning, became grave. I spoke as if to one in front of me, who had sprung up then and there in their presence.

"Since when did you ever concern yourself with such things?"

More dumfounded than ever now, and fairly dismayed as well, they turned their eyes about as if to search in me for the one who had uttered the words that were in their minds, and which had been on the tips of their tongues. How did it come? Had I really uttered them?

"Yes," I went on, and my manner was serious, "you know very well that your father left that fellow, Marco di Dio, there for all those years without molesting him. How did you happen to think of it now?"

I put a hand on Quantorzo's shoulder; my manner

was different, but none the less serious, burdened now with a painful weariness.

"I warn you," I added, "that I am not my father."

Then I turned to Firbo and laid my other hand on his shoulder:

"I want you to draw up the necessary papers at once. Immediate eviction. I am the master here, and those are my orders. And then, I want the file for my houses, with the documents on each one. Where are they?"

Plain words. Straightforward questions. Marco di Dio. Eviction. The file for the houses. The documents. Nevertheless, they did not understand me, but stood there staring at me like a couple of fools. I had to tell them a number of times that I wanted to be taken to the filing-cabinet which contained the documents that Notary Stampa needed respecting that house. Once in the room where the cabinet was, after Firbo and Quantorzo had led me there like a couple of automatons, I took each of them by the arm and put him out of the room, slamming the door on their backs. I feel sure that they stood there, on the other side of the door, for a spell, looking each other stupidly in the eye, and that one of them then said to the other:

"He must be mad!"

VI

The Theft

THAT filing-cabinet, the moment I was alone, at once laid hold of me like an incubus. I was aware, as if it had been a living thing, of the incumbering presence of the ancient and inviolate custodian, cumbersome, worm-eaten and groaning under the weight of all those documents. I looked at it, then quickly dropped my eyes and glanced around me. The window; an old straw-bottomed chair; a small table, older still, bare, black and dust-covered; there was nothing else in the room. A depressing light filtered in through the windows, which were literally plastered with dust and mildew, the bars of the iron grating outside being barely visible, along with a glimpse of the blood-colored tiles of a roof over which the window looked. The tiles of that roof, the varnished wood of those window-jambs, those panes, filthy as they were, all represented the immobile calm of inanimate objects.

I thought suddenly how my father's ring-laden hands had been raised here in this very room to take down documents from the shelves of that cabinet; I could see those fleshy hands, waxen-white and with all those rings, and with the red hairs on the back of the fingers; and I could see those blue, malicious, glasslike eyes intent upon looking for something in those bundles of papers. And then, a fresh horror, blotting out the spectre of those hands, the whole volume of my black-clad body emerged and stood there before me, forcing itself upon my gaze; I could hear the quickened breathing of that body, which had come there to rob; and the sight of those hands, opening the doors of that cabinet, sent a shudder down my spine. I gritted my teeth and shrugged my shoulders.

"Now where," I thought angrily, "among all these documents is the one I want?"

In the meanwhile, in order that I might at once be doing something, I began taking out those bundles of papers by the armful and casting them upon the little table. At a certain point, I felt my arms growing numb, and I did not know whether to laugh or to cry. What sort of jest was this, robbing myself? I turned to look about me; for of a sudden, I was no longer sure of myself here. I was about to go through with an act. But was I—I? The idea assailed me that all those *strangers* who were inseparable from myself had entered with me, and that they were about to commit this theft with my hands.

I looked at my hands. Yes, they were the same ones that I knew. But did they by any chance belong to me alone? I quickly hid them behind my back; and then, as if that were not enough, I shut my eyes. In the darkness that ensued, I was conscious of a wandering impulse of will, without any definite consistency, and I was so horrified by it that I came near to fainting physically; instinctively, I put out a hand to the table for support; I opened my eyes.

"Yes, yes!" I said, "yes, yes! Utterly illogical! This thing is utterly illogical!"

And with this, I started rummaging among those papers.

What was I rummaging for? I cannot tell you. I only know that my madness once more gave way, at a certain point, and that a yet more despairing weariness overcame me, as I found myself seated on the chair in front of that table, which was now encumbered with heaped-up papers, while my knees were weighted down by another pile. I dropped my head and wanted—I really wanted—to die, if this despair that had come upon me was to prevent my going through to the end with this unheard-of undertaking of mine.

I remember that, as I sat there with my head bowed over those papers, and with my eyes closed, possibly to keep back the tears, I heard as from an infinite distance, borne by the wind which must have come up outside, the cackling of a hen that had laid an egg. That cackling recalled for me a bit of countryside that I knew, where I had not been since the end of my boyhood days; but this impression unfortunately was impinged upon by the irritating squeak from time to time of the nearby window-shutter flapped by the wind. There came, finally, a couple of unlooked-for knocks at the door. I started up.

"Don't bother me!"

And I once more began rummaging furiously.

When at last I had found the bundle containing all the documents having to do with the house in question, I felt a sense of liberation; I leaped to my feet exultantly, but immediately afterward turned to look at the door. It was so very rapid, that change from exultation to suspicion, the suspicion that *I was seen*—I shuddered. Robber! I was robbing. I was *really* robbing. Going over and putting my shoulders against the door, I unbuttoned my waistcoat, unbuttoned the bosom of my shirt, and hid within them that sufficiently bulky bundle.

A beetle, none too steady on its legs, at that instant came crawling out from under the cabinet, directly toward the window. I was on it at once and crushed it with my foot.

With a face smeared with dirt, I stowed all the other documents helter-skelter back into the cabinet, and left the room. Luckily, Quantorzo, Firbo and all the employes had by this time gone away; there was no one there but the old watchman, who would not suspect anything. I felt, nevertheless, called upon to say something.

"Better clean up the floor in there; I just stepped on a beetle."

And I hastened out into the Via del Crocefisso, to Notary Stampa's office.

VII

The Explosion

I CAN hear still the spurt of water from an eaves-trough near the lamp, which had not been lighted yet, that stood in front of Marco di Dio's hovel, in a street that was dark before sundown; and I can see the people huddled along the walls, to be out of the rain as they watched the eviction, and other people who, under umbrellas, had paused out of curiosity at sight of the crowd and of the pitiful heap of household goods that had been set out in the downpour, in front of the door. All this was accompanied by Signora Diamante's screams, as she, all disheveled, came to the window to hurl forth certain weird imprecations of her own; and these were received with catcalls and other stupid noises by the overgrown barefoot ragamuffins who, paying no heed to the rain, were engaged in dancing about that wretched heap and splashing water from the puddles upon the curious ones, as the latter cursed them out for it roundly. And the comments that were to be heard:

"He's more disgusting than his father!"

"Out in the rain, sir! He couldn't even wait until tomorrow!"

"Treating a poor crazy man like that!"

"Usurer! Usurer!"

For I was there; yes, I was present at the eviction,

under the protection of a deputy and a couple of policemen.

"Usurer! Usurer!"

I smiled at it all. Yes, it may be that I was a trifle pale. Yet all the same, I experienced a voluptuousness that stirred my entrails, tickled my uvula and made me gulp. But in spite of this, I felt the need now and then of something on which to fix my gaze; and so, it was with a sort of lazy absent-mindedness that I kept staring at the door-moulding of that hovel, seeking thereby a little visual isolation, being certain that it would never occur to any one, at such a moment as this, to raise their eyes for the pleasure of assuring themselves that it was a very melancholy moulding indeed, to which all the noises from the street meant absolutely nothing; that peeling gray plaster affair, with perforations here and there, did not, like me, feel the need of blushing, as if for an offense against modesty, at sight of an old chamber-pot which had been set out with other objects from the hovel and exposed to the gaze of all, upon a chest of drawers, in the middle of the street.

However, this pleasurable self-removal came near costing me dear. When the eviction had been accomplished, Marco di Dio, coming out of the hovel with his wife, Diamante, and catching sight of me there in the lane, between the deputy and the two policemen, was unable to restrain himself; and as I stood there staring fixedly at that moulding, he let fly at me his old rough-caster's mallet. I should certainly have had my head crushed, if the deputy had not promptly jerked me back. Amid shouts and confusion, the two policemen darted forward to arrest the poor devil, who had been worked up to a fury at sight of me; but the crowd, which had grown by now, protected him and was about to turn on me, when a little fellow in black, down at the heels but fierce-looking, a youth from Notary Stampa's office, climbed up on a table among the household goods in the middle of the lane, and, gesticulating furiously and all but dancing, began shouting:

"Wait! Wait! Wait and hear! I come in the name of Notary Stampa! You are going to hear! Marco di Dio! Where is Marco di Dio? I come in the name of Notary Stampa to inform him that there is a donation waiting for him! That usurer, Moscarda—"

I cannot explain it, but I was trembling all over, as if in expectation of a miracle, the miracle of my own transfiguration, from one moment to another, in the sight of all. And then, without warning, my mood was hacked to a thousand bits, and my whole being was hurled violently and dispersed here and there by an explosion of ear-splitting catcalls, mingled with nameless cries and insults on the part of the whole crowd, at the mention of my name; for they, of course, were not in a position to know that it was I who had made the donation, after having so cruelly and relentlessly staged the eviction.

"Kill him! Down with him!" shouted the crowd. "Usurer! Usurer!"

Instinctively, I had raised a hand, by way of signifying that they should wait; but when I had a vision of myself in an act of supplication, I at once dropped it to my side, as that youth upon the table, waving his arms about to impose silence, went on shouting:

"No! No! You shall hear! It was he who gave it! It was he who gave the donation, at Notary Stampa's! The donation of a house to Marco di Dio!"

The crowd, at this, was amazed. But I felt distant, disillusioned, degraded. Still, that silence on the part of the crowd held me. It was as when one applies a spark to a heap of wood; for a moment, you do not see or hear anything; and then, here a wisp, there a cluster flares up; and finally, the whole bundle is crackling, and flames are licking upward through the smoke.

"He? A house? How's that? What house? Keep still! What's he saying?"

These and other similar questions began popping from the crowd; and there was a murmur, growing ever in volume and becoming more and more confused, as that notary's young man shouted out a confirmation:

"Yes, yes, a house! His house, in the Via dei Santi, No. 15. And that's not all! He's donating also ten thousand lire, for a plant and the outfitting of a laboratory!"

I was not able to see what followed; I was deprived of the pleasure through having, at that moment, to hasten somewhere else. But it is not hard for me to imagine what my pleasure would have been, had I remained.

I had to go hide myself in the entry-way of that

house in the Via dei Santi, to wait for Marco di Dio
to come and take possession. The entry-way was
barely lighted from the stair. When, with the whole
crowd at his heels, Marco di Dio opened the street
door with the key which had been turned over to
him by the notary, and caught sight of me there,
leaning against the wall like a ghost, he fell back
at first in utter disconcertion; then he shot me, from
his cruel eyes, a look which I shall never forget, and
with the snarl of a wild beast, a sound compounded
at once of sobs and laughter, he leaped upon me
frantically and began screaming at me; I could not
tell whether he meant to exalt or slay me, as he
hurled me up against the wall.

"Madman! Madman! Madman!"

And the same cry came from all the crowd in
front of the door:

"Madman! Madman! Madman!"

And all because I had wanted to prove that I could
be to others, as well as myself, something other than
what they believed me to be.

BOOK FIFTH

I

Tail Between My Legs

I was in a position to benefit, at any rate for the present, by an argument of Quantorzo's, to the effect that my father in his day had been given to "freakish indulgences" or fits of generosity like this, accompanied by a certain good-natured cruelty, and that it would never have occurred to him, Quantorzo, to suggest that my father ought to be shut up in an insane asylum or at least given a guardian, as Firbo strenuously insisted should be done in my case, by way of saving the bank's standing, which had been seriously endangered by my mad act. Just as if, good Lord, everybody in the country did not know that I had never meddled, to any extent whatsoever, in the bank's affairs. Why, then, this threatened danger to its standing? What did the bank have to do with this act of mine?

Ah, then, Quantorzo's argument, which was intended to shelter me behind my father's back, fell down. For while my father may have had these freakish spells from time to time, yet, in the transaction of business, he had always shown that he had a head upon his shoulders, which was the reason why it would never have occurred to any one to lock him up in an insane asylum or to give him a guardian; whereas, my avowed folly and complete lack of interest revealed me as nothing other than

a madman who ought to be confined, the only thing
I was good for being to tear down scandalously what
my father with so much hidden sagacity had
built up.

There was nothing to do but admit that all the
logic was on Firbo's side. But, if you please, it was
equally on Quantorzo's side, as he (as I have not
the slightest doubt he did), in a confidential ses-
sion, called Firbo's attention to the fact that, inasmuch as I was the owner of the bank, this utter
lack of business concern on my part and my foolish
actions were not to be held against me, since it was,
as a matter of fact, thanks to this that they, the two
of them, were the real, inside directors; and that,
therefore—come, come—the best thing to do was
to keep still and leave well enough alone, at least
until I might show signs of a desire to commit fresh
acts of madness.

But on the other hand and for my part, I could,
privately, have put a question to Firbo, as to
whether—beaten down as I was by all that I had
just gone through—the best thing for me to do was
not to stand with my tail between my legs, while he
and Quantorzo settled the dispute, or rather, while
it remained unsettled, as to whether Firbo's desire
to avenge himself for the insult I had offered him
in the presence of the bank's employees was to prevail, to my detriment, over the other's by no means
disinterested forbearance.

II

Dida's Laugh

ALL lumpish as I was, I had taken refuge under Dida's petticoats, in the calm, dull, lazy stupidity of her Gengè; for it seemed clear, not to her alone but to all, that if the act I had just committed was to be ascribed to madness, it must be regarded as a madness on Gengè's part, that is to say, rather, as the vaporous and momentary whim of a silly but harmless chap.

Meanwhile, as I listened to the scoldings she gave that Gengè of hers, my stomach was turned by a feeling of degradation which I am here unable to express, and the next moment, my body was shaken with bursts of laughter which I was powerless to restrain in view of the mien that I was supposed to be preserving, not one of compunction, Heaven help us! but rather that of a stubborn wretch who does not know when he is beaten, while all the time realizing that, true enough, he may have carried things a bit too far. And there was, at the same time, the fear, no longer held within bounds, which shone so startlingly from those eyes, or which occasionally burst forth from that mouth in horrible cries of atrocious despair that came from my secret and unconfessable anguish.

Yes, unconfessable; unconfessable, because a thing of my spirit only, that anguish which was

beyond the bounds of any form that I could invent
or recognize as my own, other than this one, for
example, true and tangible in my person, which my
wife was giving to that Gengè of hers, who stood
there in front of her, and who was not I; as a result,
I could no longer say who I was, nor from where or
from whom, outside of him, came that atrocious and
suffocating anguish that I knew. And in the meanwhile, held by this torment, I had become so self-
alienated as to give my body over, like a blind man,
into the hands of others, that each one might take,
of all those inseparable strangers that I bore around
within me, the one that was for him, and that he
might, if he so desired, flay it, kiss it if he liked, or
even go and shut it up in a madhouse.

"Here, Gengè. Sit down here. Over here. Look
me straight in the eyes. Why not? Don't you want
to look at me?"

Ah, what a temptation it was to take her face in
my hands and compel her to look down into the
abysmal depths of that pair of eyes, so very different
from the ones with which she wanted me to look at
her! There she was before me; she took my hair in
her hand; she sat down upon my knees; I was conscious of the weight of her body.

Who was she?

There was not the slightest doubt in her mind
that I knew who she was.

And I, all the while, was so horror-struck by her
eyes, by her assured and smiling gaze upon me—a
horror of those cool hands that stroked me, in the
certainty that I was as those eyes beheld me; a

horror of the whole of that body, which was a weight upon my knees, so confident in its self-abandonment to me, without the remotest suspicion that it was not in reality giving itself to me, that I, as I clasped it in my arms, was not clasping in that body one who belonged wholly to me, but rather, a strange woman, to whom I was unable in any fashion to explain what she was, since she was for me no more and no less than what I saw and touched in her: this woman —here—with this hair—and these eyes—and this mouth which I kissed with love's own fire, while she kissed mine with a fire so different from my own, and immeasurably far away; it was as if all for her, sex, nature, imagery, and the feel of things, all the thoughts and affections that went to make up her spirit, memories, tastes, and the mere contact of my scraggly cheek with her delicate one, were wholly and utterly different; we were two strangers, two strangers—the horror of the thing—locked in an embrace, strangers not merely one to the other, but each to himself, in that body which the other clasped.

You, I know, have never experienced this horror; for the reason that all you have done, ever, has been to clasp in your arms the whole of your world, in the person of the woman who is yours, without the faintest suspicion that she all the while has been embracing her world in you, which is another one, one where you may not enter. Ah, well, if you would like to feel this horror, you have but to think for a moment—what shall I say?—of any trifle whatsoever, of something that pleases you and does not please her, a color, a taste on the tongue, an opinion on something or other; you have but to do this, and it will at once occur to you, at least superficially, that there is such a thing as a diversity of tastes, of perceptions and of opinions, that her eyes, even while you are looking at her, do not see in you, as do your own, the things that you see in her, and that the world, life and the reality of things as it is for you, as you touch it, do not exist for her, who sees and touches another reality in those same things, and in you yourself, and in herself, without your being able to say how it happens, since for her it is that one, and she is unable to conceive that there may possibly be another for you.

It cost me much to conceal the cold malignity that was ever more and more congealing in my mind, as I perceived that Dida, at bottom, however she might force herself to put a stern face on the matter, was laughing over the brutal pastime in which her Gengè had been indulging; she obviously did not pause to reflect that everyone might not understand that all he had wanted to do was to play a practical joke, no more.

"But just think a minute, whether that's any kind of joke to play! Evicting them in the rain like that, and being there yourself to stir up their indignation, you big silly! They might have killed you for the moment!"

As she said this, she turned her head to hide a smile which had been provoked by the sight of this sulkiness on my part. This sulkiness in the person of her Gengè, as she saw him there before her, and as she pictured him at the time of the eviction, when all were so indignant with him, impressed her as being pure spite, nothing other than a comical feeling of spite on the part of her "big silly," and all on account of a joke that had miscarried and been misunderstood.

"What did you expect, anyway? Did you think they were going to laugh at that crazy fellow's rage, while you were setting his junk out in the street in the rain? And to think—just look at him, will you?—that he had that donation under his hat all the time! Oh, I'm afraid Signor Firbo's right, after all! It's a thing that calls for the madhouse, a joke in as bad taste as that; and think of the price you have to pay for it. Off with you, off! Here's Bibi; take her out for a while."

I saw the bitch's red leash being put into my hand; and I saw my wife bend down, with that readiness with which women do bend over the things that are their own, gently to adjust the muzzle on Bibi's little snout. I remained standing there like a fool.

"What are you doing? Aren't you going?"

"I'm going."

As the door closed behind me, I stopped on the stair-landing and leaned against the wall; I felt like dropping down on the top step and never rising again.

III

I Have a Talk With Bibi

I FIND myself slinking along the street walls, no longer knowing which way to look or what face to put on the matter, with that bitch at my heels. The dog appears to be doing its best to give me to understand that, if I do not wish to go, neither does she care to come with me; she puts down her little paws and has to be dragged, until I become angry and give her a fierce tug, at the risk of breaking that red leash of hers.

I seek hiding, a short distance from the house, within the enclosure of a property that has been sold for a house that is going up there, a big house and no telling how ugly, to judge from its neighbors. The foundation has been partly excavated, but the mounds of earth have not yet been carted away; and scattered about in the thick grass which has sprung up are the building-stones, old-looking and crumbling before they are used.

I sit upon one of these stones and gaze at the wall of the house next door, which looms tall, white, and etched against the blue. Left bare like that, without a window, that wall in the beating sun is blinding. I drop my eyes to the patch of shade here on the vagrant grass, which sends up a rich, warm odor into the pregnant silence, broken only by the hum of minute insects; a big black fly, irritated by my

172

presence, settles buzzingly on me; I observe Bibi, sitting on her haunches in front of me with her ears stuck out in deluded suspense, as if to ask me why it was we have come here, to this out-of-the-way place, where, among other things— Ah, yes, at night, some passer-by—

"Yes, Bibi," I say to her. "That stench—I smell it, too. But to me, you know, it is the least offensive one that can come to me henceforth from men. It is of the body. The one that exhales from the soul and its needs is worse, Bibi. And you are really to be envied, since you can have no intimation of it."

I draw her to me by her two front paws and go on talking to her like this:

"Do you want to know why I came to hide away here? Ah, Bibi, because people stare at me. That is a vice that people have, and you cannot cure them of it. The only thing to do is for all of us to cure ourselves of the vice of taking down the street, for a walk, a body that is subject to being stared at. Ah, Bibi, Bibi, what am I going to do? I cannot stand being stared at any more. Not even by you. I am even afraid when you stare at me the way you are doing now. No one doubts what he sees, and each one goes walking through the world of objects assured that they appear to others as they are to him; and do you imagine for a minute there is any one who stops to think of you animals, as you gaze at men and things with those silent eyes of yours? Who knows in what manner you see them, or how they look to you? I have lost, I have lost forever my reality, and that which lies behind all things in the eyes of others, Bibi! No sooner do I touch it than it vanishes. For the reason that, under this very touch of mine, I presuppose the reality that others attribute to me, and which I do not know, and never can know. And so it comes—do you see it all?—that I—the one who is talking to you now—the one who now holds your two paws up from the earth like this—the very words that I am saying to you—I do not know, Bibi, I really do not know, who it is that is uttering them."

The poor little beast gave an unexpected start at this point, in an effort to free her two paws from my hands. I did not pause to reflect as to whether or not this start may have been due to the terror inspired by what I had just said to her; but in order not to injure her paws, I let them go, and she at once fled barking after a white cat that she had glimpsed in the grass at the other end of the enclosure. The red leash, however, dragging between her legs as she ran, caught on a twig and gave her such a jerk as to throw her over backwards and send her rolling all in a heap. Trembling with rage, she got to her feet and stood there, squarely on all-fours, not knowing where to find an outlet for her interrupted fury; she looked in this direction and that; the cat was no longer in sight.

She sneezed.

I could laugh, first at that chase of hers, then at her backward tumble, and now at seeing her standing there like that; I threw back my head and called her to me. She came, lightly and gracefully, almost dancing on her slender legs; when she had come up to me, she lifted her two front paws to lay them upon one of my knees, as if she wished to go on with a pleasing conversation that had been broken off in the middle. And that was why, as I spoke to her, I scratched her head behind the ears.

"No, no, Bibi, that is enough," I said. "Let us rather shut our eyes."

I took her head in my hands; but the little creature struggled to be free, and I let her go. Shortly afterward, as she lay stretched out at my feet, with her tiny snout resting on her two front paws, I heard her breathing heavily; it was as if she had had all that she could bear of weariness and vexation of spirit, as if the load were all too great, even in the life of a poor little, pretty little, much petted she-dog.

IV

Others' Vision

"WHY is it, when one thinks of killing himself, that
he imagines himself as being dead, no longer to himself, but to others?"

Bloated and livid, like the corpse of a drowned
man, my torment came up to the surface with this
question, after I had been sunk for more than an
hour in meditation, there in that enclosure, considering whether this were not perhaps the moment
to have done with it all, not so much by way of free-
ing myself from my torment, as by way of affording a charming gratification to that grudge which
I knew that many bore me, or even by way of affording a proof of that imbecility which so many others
attributed to me.

Well, then, amid the various images of a violent
death such as could come to me, which, might I suppose, were the unforeseen ones that would leap up,
amid the general consternation and amazement,
in the minds of my wife, Quantorzo, Firbo, and all
my many, many other acquaintances? Constrain-
ing myself to reply to this question, I felt more than
ever unequal to it, since I could not but realize that
in my eyes there was not, to tell the truth, any power
of vision for myself, such as would enable me to
state in some fashion or other how it was I saw
myself without the vision of others, or to imagine,

so far as my own body or anything else was concerned, how others might see them; the conclusion
being, that my eyes in themselves, apart from the
vision of others, would no longer really have known
what it was they beheld.

A shiver ran down my spine at a distant memory
that now came back to me, of the time when I was
a boy and when, walking deep in thought over the
countryside, I had suddenly discovered that I was
lost, without a hint as to my whereabouts, in a
remote and gloomy solitude; I recalled the fear that
came over me, which at the time I had not been
able to explain. It was this: the horror of something which, from one moment to the next, might
be revealed to me and me alone, beyond the range
of others' vision. For always, when we chance to
come upon something which we suppose that others
have never seen, do we not run to call someone, to
come at once and see it with us?

"My God, what's that?"

Where the vision of others does not come to our
succor, to build up in us in some manner the reality
of what we see, our eyes are no longer aware what
it is that meets their gaze; our consciousness
vanishes, since what we believe to be our most
intimate possession, our consciousness, means
simply *others in us,* and we in ourselves are unable
to perceive it.

I leaped to my feet, terrified. I had known, I had
known the solitude that was mine; but only now
did I feel and touch the horror that confronted me
in every object that I saw—my hand, if I held it up

and looked at it.   For others' vision is not and cannot be to our eyes anything but an illusion, and this
was an illusion in which I no longer could believe.
In a total daze, and fancying that I beheld my own
horror in the eyes of the bitch, as she, too, started
up and fixed her gaze upon me, I gave her a kick,
simply to get that horror out of my sight; but at the
sound of her heart-rending yelps, I quickly and
despairingly took her head in my hands.

"I'm going mad!" I cried, "I'm going mad!"

I cannot say how it was, but in that despairing
gesture I saw myself again; and with this, the tears
which had been about to burst forth were trans-
formed into a startling peal of laughter, as I called
the poor half-crippled Bibi over to me and myself
began limping as a jest, a prey all the while to a
fierce and maniacal merriment.   I told her that I
had been playing, playing, and that I wanted to go
on playing.   The little creature sneezed, as if to say:
"I refuse! I refuse!"

"Ah, so you refuse, do you, Bibi; you refuse?"

And then, I started sneezing just to keep her company, repeating with every sneeze:

"I refuse! I refuse!"

V

The Delightful Game

"KICK her? I kick that poor little beast? I?"

No, no! Not I! A certain overgrown, shame-faced country lad might have done so, on account of some strange fear or other that had laid hold of him, a fear of everything and nothing, a nothing that might in an unlooked-for manner become *something* which he then would be the only one to behold. But here in the city, now, here in the street, there was no longer any danger of that. What the deuce! Each one snug in his illusion of another, so that he might be assured that all the others were wrong, should they tell him no, that each one was not as another saw him. I felt like shouting to all the world: "Come! Come! Let's play the game! Let's play the game!"

I also felt like making a sign to anyone who by chance stood looking out of a window. Come! Come! Even to the point of opening that window and leaping out.

"A delightful game! And who knows, my dear sir, my dear madam, what charming surprises you would encounter, if after having thus flung your-selves down from every illusion that you possess concerning yourselves, you could come back for a fraction of a second from the dead, to view in the illusion of others yet living that world in which you imagined that you lived! Ah, ha!"

179

The unfortunate part was that, still alive, I had to witness this game among the other living, although I was unable to fathom it. And this impossibility of fathoming it, while all the time knowing that it was there, where everybody could see it, exasperated my mood of maniacal mirth to the point of savage fury. That kick which I had let fly at that poor little beast, simply because she had looked at me, I now felt, God forgive me, like bestowing upon all mankind.

VI

Multiplication and Subtraction

COMING back home, I found Quantorzo there, in a
serious confab with my wife, Dida. There they
were, so primly sure of themselves, seated in the
little half-lighted drawing-room, the one a dark,
heavy figure, wallowing in the depths of the green
divan, the other slender and white, in a gown that
was all frills and furbelows and which spread out
for three-quarters of its bulk over a neighboring
easy chair, and with a glint of sunlight on her
throat. They had certainly been talking of me; for
when they saw me coming in, they both at once exclaimed: "Oh, here he is now!"

In view of the fact that there were two of them
who saw me enter, the temptation came to me to
turn and look for the other one who had entered
with me, knowing very well, as I did, that my
paternal friend Quantorzo's "dear Vitangelo" was
also in me, as was my wife Dida's "Gengè," and
that the whole of me together for Quantorzo was
none other than that same "dear Vitangelo," and
for Dida, none other than her "Gengè." There were,
accordingly, two, not in their eyes, but only for me
who knew that, to this pair, I was *one* and *one;* all
of which, for me, went to make not a *more* but a *less,*
in so far as it implied that, in their eyes, I as I was
no one.

181

In their eyes alone?   The same was true of myself as, at this moment, in my spiritual solitude,
without any apparent consistency, I came to know
the horror of seeing my own body as being in itself
that of a nobody, in the differing and incoer-
cible reality which those two all the while were
bestowing upon me.

"Whom are you looking for?" my wife asked me,
upon seeing me turn.   I hastened to reply, with a
smile, "Ah, no one, my dear, no one.   We are all
here, aren't we?"

She naturally did not know what I meant by that
"no one" whom I had looked for at my side, but
believed that my "We are all here, aren't we?"
referred to the two of them, being very sure that in
that little drawing-room, we were three and not
nine—or rather, eight, seeing that I, to myself, no
longer counted.   I mean to say:

1) Dida as she was to herself;
2) Dida as she was to me;
3) Dida as she was to Quantorzo;
4) Quantorzo as he was to himself;
5) Quantorzo as he was to Dida;
6) Quantorzo as he was to me;
7) Dida's dear Gengè;
8) Quantorzo's dear Vitangelo.

What a charming conversation there was going
to be, here in this drawing-room, among these
eight who believed themselves three!

VII

But All the While, I Was Saying to Myself

(GOOD LORD, and can it be they do not feel their self-assurance fading away, as they see themselves being stared at by these eyes of mine, which *do not know what they see?*

Pause for a moment and stare at someone who is performing the most ordinary and obvious act in life, stare at him in such a manner as to cause the suspicion to arise in his mind that what he is doing is not clear to us, and that it may similarly not be clear to himself; do this, and his self-assurance at once is overcast and begins to waver. No crowd could be more disconcerting than that pair of unseeing eyes, eyes that do not see us, or which do not see the same thing that we do.

"Why do you stare like that?"

And no one stops to think that this is the way in which we all ought always to stare, each with eyes horror-filled at his own inescapable solitude.)

VIII

To the Quick

QUANTORZO, the truth is, at once began to be upset, the moment his eyes confronted mine; he began to ramble in his talk, to such an extent as involuntarily to raise a hand now and then, as if to say, "No, wait—"

I was not long, however, in discovering my mistake. He rambled like that, not because my gaze had shaken his self-assurance, but because he thought he had made out from my eyes that I already grasped the real object of this call of his, which was, in accordance with an understanding with Firbo, to bind me hand and foot, upon the ground that it was out of the question for me to continue being the bank's director, if I expected to take upon myself the right to commit other unpredictable and arbitrary acts, for which neither he nor Firbo could afford to assume the responsibility.

Being certain, then, of this, I resolved to disconcert him, not, however instantaneously, as I had done the other time, by talking and gesticulating like a madman in his and Firbo's presence, but in an opposite fashion. I had a fancy for seeing how he would carry it off, after having come here with his mind so made up, a fancy, I will state, which had been inspired by that bellicosely determined attitude of his. I wanted to prove to myself yet once again, although there was no need of my doing so, how a mere trifle, nothing at all, would suffice to cause that determination to crumble—a word I might say, the tone in which I might say it—how this would serve to divert him, cause him to change his mind, and with his mind, of necessity, the whole of that solid-seeming reality of his, as he felt it within and saw and touched it outside himself.

No sooner had he done telling me that Firbo, especially, was unable to rest easy over what I had done, than I put on a fatuous smile to anger him, and asked, "More of that?"

He was properly angered.

"More of that? Do you know what you did, old man? You left all those documents in the filing-cabinet in such a mess that it will easily take us a couple of months to put them in order again."

I became very serious at this, as I turned to Dida:

"You see, my dear? And you thought it was a joke."

There was a sudden uncertainty in the look that Dida gave me; she then glanced at Quantorzo; then back at me.

"Well, what in the world have you done?" she asked at last, in a tone of apprehension.

I raised my hand as a sign for her to wait. Then, graver than ever, I turned to Quantorzo.

"So, Signor Firbo found the mess in the filing-cabinet, did he? And how does it come, it does not occur to you to ask me what I found there?"

Quantorzo, at this point, began floundering about on the divan and batted his eyelids a score of times,

as if in an instinctive effort to overcome the daze
that had settled on him, not so much as a result of
the question as by reason of the tone of suspicion
in which I had flung it out.

"What—what did you find?" he stammered.

I gave him a quick reply, accompanying my words
with a gesture: "A handful of dust; like that!"

They gazed into each other's eyes with astonishment; my tone of voice excluded any belief that I
had said this thing, so silly in itself, out of silliness.

"A handful of dust?" Quantorzo repeated, still in
a daze. "What is the meaning of that?"

"Well! the meaning of that is that those documents have been left lying there for all these years!
A handful, I am telling you, a handful of dust. One
house unrented; and the other one—who knows how
long it has been since any rent was collected for it!"

Quantorzo—which was something I did not expect—was apparently more amazed than ever at
this.

"Ah," he said, "and so you're raking up the matter
of the houses, are you; to give them away?"

"No, my dear fellow," I forthwith shouted back
at him, growing a bit warm under the collar, with
a heat that was, I admit, partly feigned, but which
was also partly real. "No, my dear fellow. I am
doing it to show you how very, very mistaken you
are with regard to me, you and Firbo and all the
rest of you!"

Quantorzo—and this time, I did expect it—strove
to rise to this.

"But what did you observe? Please be so good as

to tell me! The dust on the filing-cabinet, that's what you observed!"

"And my hands," I hurriedly added, I do not know why, as I held them out before me. My voice was such as to awake in me an impulsive shudder, as I mentally saw myself in that little room where the cabinet was, in the act of lifting up my hands to rob myself of that document, after I had there conjured up the picture of my father's hands, white, fleshy, ring-laden, and with the red hairs on the back of the fingers.

"I come to the bank," I went on, surprised, amid the growing bewilderment of the other two, by a feeling of weariness and nausea, "I come to the bank only when you summon me to give my signature; but I would have you note that I do not need to come to the bank to know all that is going on there."

I glanced at Quantorzo out of the corner of my eye; he looked very pale to me. (But mark you, I am all the time speaking of my Quantorzo; it may be that Dida's did not; or if it did seem to Dida that he turned a trifle pale, she may have attributed this to indignation rather than fear, although I could have sworn it was the latter.) In any event, his hands went up to his bosom in an instinctive gesture, and his eyes were fairly popping out of his head:

"Ah, so you're playing the spy, then, are you? So you don't trust us, is that it?"

"It is not that I do not trust you; it is not that; and it is not that I am playing the spy," I hastened to reassure him. "I observe as an outsider the results of your operations, that's all. But answer me one thing: you and Firbo, are you not, in your transaction of business, carrying out my father's wishes?"

"Scrupulously!"

"I have no doubt of it. But you for your part are protected by the positions you hold, one of you being the director and the other the legal adviser. My father, unfortunately, is no longer there. What I want to know is, who is responsible to the public for what the bank does?"

"What do you mean, who is responsible?" said Quantorzo. "Why, we are! We are! And it is just because we are responsible that we want to be sure that you will not come meddling again, doing certain things which, to put it mildly, are ill-advised!"

I raised a finger in negation.

"That's not true," I said to him, placidly. "Not if you are scrupulously carrying out my father's wishes, as you say. I, in any event, am the one to whom you should answer, in case you are not carrying them out; I am the one who has the right to demand an accounting of you. And now, I am asking you: who is it that is responsible to the public? It is I, who sign your papers for you—it is I! It is I! You want my signature, right enough, on everything you do; and yet, you deny me your approval for one thing I do; that, I perceive, is the pass to which things have come."

He must have been quite thoroughly browbeaten;

for at this juncture, I saw him bounce lightly three times upon the divan.

"I like that!" he exclaimed. "I like that! I like that! If you want to know, it's because ours are the bank's normal transactions! Whereas, that act of yours, if you will pardon me—you force me to say it—was that of a madman! a madman!"

I leaped to my feet and pointed a forefinger against his bosom, like a weapon.

"So, you think I'm mad, do you?"

"Why, no!" he said, swiftly paling under the threat of that finger.

"So, you don't, eh?" I cried, holding him fixedly with my eyes. "Good, then, that little matter is settled between us, anyway!"

Quantorzo, half up in the air as it were, was wavering by this time; not because he then and there had conceived a fresh doubt as to my sanity, not that at all; it was that he did not understand my reason for insisting upon settling the point that he did not regard me as mad; and in his uncertainty, fearing a trap on my part, he all but repented having said no in the first place, and now, with the beginning of a smile on his face, attempted to unsay it:

"No, wait—but you must agree—"

Ah, but it was going off charmingly—charmingly! Dida, with knit brows, was now glancing first at me and then at Quantorzo; it was plain that she no longer knew what to think either of him or of me. That outburst of mine, that ticklish question, were for her, it must be understood, an outburst and a question on the part of her Gengè; and coming from him, they were quite incomprehensible, unless it could be that Quantorzo there present and Signor Firbo had been guilty of some dereliction sufficiently grave to render her Gengè at this minute—good Heavens!—quite unrecognizable; and so it was, in view of Quantorzo's momentary daze, that outburst and that question had all the effect of causing her to doubt, more than ever before, the staid sagacity of that friend of hers, the respectable Quantorzo. This doubt was so openly mirrored in her eyes that Quantorzo, as he turned to her in his half-smiling attempt to take back what he had said, grew more dazed than ever, as he suddenly became aware that there was lacking at his side that supporting opinion upon which he had thought up to then that he assuredly could rely.

I burst into a laugh; but neither one nor the other of them guessed the cause. I was tempted to lay hold of them and shake them, as I screamed in their faces, "Do you see? Do you see! How, then, can you be so sure, since the least impression, at any moment, is all that is needed to make you doubt both yourselves and others?"

"Let's drop it!" I broke in, with an irate gesture, by way of signifying to them that any opinion that might be formed of me or of my mental sanity was no longer, at any rate for the time being, of the slightest importance. "Answer me. I saw down at the bank some scales, large and small. You employ them, I believe, for weighing pledges? But tell me something—yes, you, upon your conscience—did you ever weigh, with the scales of others, those things which you term the bank's normal transactions?"

At this question, Quantorzo darted another
glance around, as if he were being treacherously
put to it by others as well as by me.

"Upon my conscience? How is that?"

"I suppose you think that conscience has nothing
to do with it," was my speedy rejoinder. "Ah, I
understand! And perhaps, you think that the same
is true of my own, in view of the fact that I've left
it down at the bank all these years, to be administered, along with the rest of my inheritance, in
accordance with my father's wishes."

"But the bank—" Quantorzo started to object.
I burst out again.

"The bank—the bank— That's all you can think
of, the bank. But I, as it happens, outside the bank,
have to hear myself called a usurer!"

At this unlooked-for issue, Quantorzo in turn
leaped to his feet, as if I had just uttered the most
frightful of blasphemies or been guilty of the
grossest brutality; he was looking for a way out.

"Good God!" he exclaimed, with his arms
upraised; and then again, "Good God!" And
falling back with his head in his hands, he looked
at my wife, as much as to say, "Do you hear that?
Do you hear this childish talk of his? And I thought
he had something serious to say to me!"

He shook me by the arms, as if to shake me out
of that daze (I was the one who was dazed now)
which had been instinctively produced by this
passionate bit of acting on his part.

"Do you mean to tell me," he shouted, "that you really give that a serious thought? Bah! Be off with you! Be off with you!"

And by way of having his revenge, he pointed me out to my wife, who laughed— Ah, how she laughed, laughed as if her sides would burst—no doubt on account of what I had just said, but also, it may be, on account of the effect which my words had had upon Quantorzo, not to mention the bewilderment which had subsequently taken possession of me, and which assuredly revived in her mind and left with her a most vivid picture of her dear Gengè and his well-known but darling foolishness.

However this may be, at the sound of that laugh, I all at once felt stabbed to the quick, a thing that I should never have expected could happen to me at the moment, considering my state of mind; for I had partly instigated this conversation and partly let it drift; but now, I had been stabbed to an inner point of my being, I could not say what or where. It had been so clear to me up to then that, in the presence of these two, I—as I—was non-existent, and that those really there were the "Gengè" of the one and the "dear Vitangelo" of the other, in whom it was impossible for me to feel myself alive. But now, as I say, apart from any image I might shape that would depict me to myself as a living being, as someone even to myself, apart from any image of myself that I could conceive as existing for others, the "quick" in me had been so palpably wounded that the light of my eyes went out.

"Stop that laughing!" I cried, in such a voice to

my wife's ears that the latter, as she looked at me (and who knows what a face she must have seen on me), at once became dumb and lost countenance completely. I followed it up immediately.

"And you listen to what I'm telling you," I said, whirling on Quantorzo. "I want the bank closed this very evening."

"Closed? What do you mean?"

"Closed! Closed!" I insisted, towering above him. "I want it closed! Am I the proprietor, or am I not?"

"No!" He bridled up. "No, old chap, what do you mean, the proprietor! You are not the only one, not by any means!"

"And who are the other ones? You and Signor Firbo?"

"And your father-in-law! And any number of others!"

"Yet the bank is in my name only!"

"No, it's in the name of your father, who founded it!"

"Well, then, I want that name taken off!"

"Taken off! It's impossible!"

"It is, is it? Stop and think a minute! Am I not the proprietor of my own name? Of my father's name?"

"No, because that name is a part of the bank's charter; it is the name of the bank, which is your father's creature as much as you are! And it bears his name by the very same right!"

"Ah, is that so?"

"Yes, it's so!"

"And what about the money, his own money that my father put into it? Was it to the bank or to me that my father left his money?"

"To you, invested in the bank's operations."

"And supposing that I do not care to leave it there any longer? Supposing that I wish to take it out and invest it elsewhere, as I may see fit, have I not the right to do so?"

"But you will ruin the bank, if you do that!"

"What difference do you think that makes to me? I don't want to hear any more about it, I tell you!"

"But it makes a difference to others, let me tell you! You will be ruining others, yourself, your wife, your father-in-law!"

"Nothing of the sort! The others can do as they like; they can continue keeping their money there; I'm taking mine out!"

"Do you want to throw us into bankruptcy, then?"

"I don't give a hang about that! I know what I want—what I *want,* do you understand? I want to withdraw my money, and that is all there is to it!"

I can see now that violent altercations such as these, with their thrusts and counter-thrusts, are really and truly boxing matches between two opposing wills, each of which in turn is seeking to deliver a knockout blow to the other, striking, parrying, striking back, each certain that a well-aimed punch should be able to floor the other; until each of them, from the sturdy resistance with which the other returns his pommelings, becomes more and more convinced of the futility of keeping the thing

up, since his adversary will not yield. The most
ridiculous thing of all is that, accompanying the
wrathful words, or better, screams, real fists are
spontaneously raised to the adversary's snout,
without however touching it, while teeth are
gnashed, noses are curled, eyebrows are huddled,
and the body trembles all over.

With that last volley of "I want," "I want," "I
want," three times repeated, I must have beaten
down Quantorzo's resistance. I saw him bring his
hands together, as if he were praying:

"But if one might at least know your reasons?
On the spur of the moment, like this?"

As I saw him in that attitude, I had a feeling akin
to dizziness. I at once realized that to explain
then and there, to him and to my wife, who stood
hanging upon my words, the one imploringly, the
other anxiously and terrifiedly, the motives that lay
behind my headstrong resolve, one of so great a
gravity for all concerned, was a thing of which I was
not capable. I could feel at that instant how tangled
those inner motives were, how subtle and contorted
by my many long fits of meditation; and so far as
that goes, they were no longer clear even to myself,
agitated and wrath-torn as I was, in that dark light
which glowed with so terrible a fixity, and which I
had come upon thus solitarily; while there was
nothing but darkness for all the others, who went
on living blindly and securely in the habitual
plenitude of their emotions. At the same time, I
realized that, by revealing so much as a single one
of mine, I should appear hopelessly mad to each

of this pair—for example, the fact that, up to a short while back, *I never had seen myself* as they had always seen me, that is, as one who continued to go on living tranquilly if whimsically upon the usurious proceeds of that bank, without having openly to acknowledge the fact. I had barely so much as hinted it in their presence; and lo, to each of them it had seemed an ingenuous dodge, so unlikely as to arouse the one to that comically passionate bit of acting and to evoke from the other that interminable peal of laughter. How, then, was I to tell them that it was precisely upon this "ingenuous dodge," so incredible a one in their eyes, that I was resting the whole burden of my resolve? But supposing that I had always been a usurer, always, even before I was born? Had I not glimpsed myself upon the main street of madness, setting out to commit an act which in the eyes of all must have appeared as one opposed to and inconsistent with myself? Had I not done this, flinging out from me my will, like a pocket-handkerchief? And had not I myself been brought to the realization that the usurer, Signor Vitangelo Moscarda, while he might go mad, might not in any way destroy himself?

Very well; but this was, exactly, the "quick" which had been stabbed in me, the thing that blinded me and which, at that moment, deprived me of all comprehension. A usurer, no. That usurer, a thing which I to myself had never been, I would no longer be to others, either, even though it meant bringing down in ruins upon my head everything that went to make up my life. There was, then, one feeling left in me, this one, well cemented by the power of will that came to me (although I up to that time had recognized it with diffidence and apprehension) from that self-same and consistent solidity of others, deadened and locked within itself like a stone. This was as much as my wife needed. Taking advantage of my un- anticipated bewilderment, she broke out again, commanding her Gengè to have done once and for all with those ridiculous domineering airs that he was trying to give himself. So saying she came toward me, almost with her face in her hands; that was all, and the light of my eyes went out again. Seizing her by the wrists and shaking her, I flung her backward and hurled her to a sitting posture upon the chair:

"That's enough of your Gengè! He's not I! He's not I! He's not I! Let's hear no more about that marionette! I want what I want; and what I want shall be done!"

I spun around on Quantorzo:

"Do you understand?"

He stormed out of the room.

BOOK SIXTH

BOOK SIXTH

I

Face-to-Face

A SHORT while later, locked in my room like a wild animal in a cage, I found myself panting still as a result of that violence which (for the first time) I had used upon my wife; I was unable to overcome the vision of her airy, white-clad, fluttering form, shattered to bits it seemed as, seizing her by the wrists, I shook her and, with a backward thrust, hurled her down upon the chair. Ah, how airy she was in that white dress of hers with all the furbelows on it, as I so violently and brutally assaulted her! Broken now like a fragile doll which had been cast down in a rage, a doll that I should certainly never be able to put together again. And all my life long, that portion of my life which I had spent with her, what a time I had had playing with that doll, broken in pieces now, perhaps forever.

The vivid shuddering horror inspired by my violence was evident in my hands, which were trembling still. I became aware, however, that this horror was due not so much to the violence I had exerted as it was to the blind upward surge within me of a feeling and a will which had ended by *giving body* to me: a bestial body, which had struck terror and endowed my hands with violence.

I was becoming "one"—

I.

I who now willed myself thus.

I who now felt myself thus.

At last!

No longer a usurer (have done with that bank!), and no longer Gengè (have done with that marionette!).

But my heart kept on thumping in my bosom. It took my breath away. I opened and shut my hands, sinking the nails into my flesh. Almost without knowing it, I was clawing one palm with my other hand, as I paced up and down the room, champing like a horse that will not suffer the bit. I was raving.

But I, one, who? Who?

No longer Gengè.

Another. But what other? What other had I within me, save this torment, which revealed me to myself as none and a hundred-thousand?

This new will of mine, this new feeling might surge up blindly from that "quick" inside me which had been stabbed, and which I was unable to locate; but they at once came tumbling down under the terrible fixity of that dark-gleaming light which I had discovered. I was looking, nevertheless, by way of piecing myself together, for an intimation of something which might enable me, with a drop of blood from that wound and with that bit of lacerated, macerated feeling, to erect the unhinged skeleton of the bit of will that was left me. Oh, I was a poor little, meager little man, always terror-struck by the look in others' eyes, with a satchel in his hand containing the money derived from the

liquidation of the bank. And how was I to go on
keeping that money now? Had I by any chance
earned it by my own labor? I had withdrawn it
from the bank, in order that it might not draw any
more usurious interest; but was that by any chance
sufficient to cleanse it of the taint from its source?
What then? Throw it away? And how was I to
live? Of what work was I capable? And Dida?

She, too—I was conscious of it, now that I no
longer had her in the house with me—she, too, was
a bit of *quick* in me. I loved her, notwithstanding
the torture that came to me from the absolute
awareness of not, in my own body, belonging to
myself as the object of her love. Yet I could savor
all the sweetness that came to this body from her
love, in the blind voluptuousness of an embrace;
even if, at times, I was almost tempted to strangle
her, as I saw her moist and quivering lips torn between a desire to smile and a longing to sigh, and
as I beheld, trembling there, a stupid name: *Gengè*

II

In the Void

I WAS struck by the motionless suspense of all the objects in the drawingroom, when, as if lured by the silence that had fallen there, I came back into it: that easy chair, where she had sat; that divan, upon which Quantorzo had floundered about; that little bright lacquer gold-work table, and the other chairs, and the curtains—they all gave me so horrible an impression of a void that I turned instead to look at the servants, Diego and Nina, who had come to inform me that their mistress had gone off with Signor Quantorzo, leaving orders that all her wardrobe should be collected, packed in trunks and sent to her father's house; the two of them were standing there now, gazing at me in a dumfounded manner, wide-eyed and gaping-mouthed. Their presence irritated me.

"Very well," I shouted, "see that her orders are carried out."

An order to be carried out was already something, even in this void, for others. And it was something for me, too, if it enabled me for the moment to rid myself of this pair.

When I was alone, I felt of a sudden strangely hilarious, as I thought, "I am free! She has gone away!" Yet I could not believe it was true. I had the extremely curious impression that she had

204

merely gone off by way of affording me a test of the
correctness of my discovery, one which assumed for
me an importance so vast and unqualified that everything else by comparison could have but a minor
and relative importance, even if it cost me my wife,
even because it cost me my wife.

"Just see whether it's true or not!"

It was only the test that was terrible. All the
rest—Ah, yes, away with it!—even seemed ridiculous, if one looked at it that way: her traipsing off
with Quantorzo like that, and my becoming worked
up over the gross stupidity of those who believed me
to be a usurer. But how then? Had I been brought
to this? To the point where I could no longer take
anything seriously? And the stab which I had experienced a short while back, which had led to that
violent outburst?

That was all very well. But where was the stab?
In me? If I touched myself, if I rubbed my hands
together, if I said "I"—but to whom was I saying it?
For whose benefit? I was alone. In all the world,
I was alone. For myself, I was alone. And in the
instantaneous shudder which now shot up to the
roots of my hair, I knew eternity and all the
frigidity of that infinite solitude. To whom was I
to say "I"? Of what use to say "I," if one were to
be at once caught up into the horror of this infinite
void, this infinite solitude?

III

I Continue to Make Matters Worse

MY FATHER-IN-LAW came to look me up the next morning.

I should first tell you (but I shall not tell you) to what point I had been carried by my imagination; I had spent a good part of the night in a frenzy, in an impetuous attempt to deduce the consequences of that position into which I had put myself, not alone with regard to others, but also with respect to myself. I had aroused myself from a brief and leaden slumber with a sensation of the hostile gravity of all things, even of the water that I held in the palm of my hand with which to wash myself, and of the towels which I afterward employed. And then, upon being informed that I had a caller, I felt a sudden lightness come over me, as a result of an immediate re-awakening of that mood of mirthful madness which, by good fortune, still swept my spirit now and then like a beneficent breeze. I sent the towels flying, as I said to Nina: "Very well, very well. Show him into the drawing-room and tell him that I will be down at once."

I glanced at myself in the clothespress mirror with an irresistible self-confidence; I even winked an eye by way of signifying to that Moscarda there that we two understood each other, all the while, marvelously well. And it is but the truth I am tell-

ing you, when I say that he winked back, by way
of confirming that understanding.

(You, I know, will inform me that this was due
to the fact that the Moscarda in the mirror there
was I; and by so doing, you will be proving to me
yet one more time that you know nothing whatever
about it. It was not I, I can assure you of that.
This is evidenced by the fact that when, a moment
later, before going out of the room, I turned my
head a trifle to have a look at him in the mirror, he
was already another person, even to me, with a
satanic smile in his keen and brightly gleaming eyes.
You would have been terrified by it, but not I; for
the reason that I knew him; and I gave him a wave
of the hand. He waved back at me in turn.)

All this as a beginning. The comedy was to follow
in the drawingroom, with my father-in-law.

With four of us present?

No.

You shall see how many varied Moscardas, all
differing from the self that I had been, I was to
amuse myself by producing that morning.

IV

Doctor, Lawyer, Merchant, Chief?

IT WAS undoubtedly my father-in-law who occasioned this unhoped-for re-awakening of my mood, owing to that possibly disrespectful (Heaven knows, it was) reality which I up to this time had attributed to him, that of being a very stupid and invariably self-satisfied individual.

He was exceedingly well-groomed, not only as to his clothes, but to the part of his hair and his mustache, which was combed to the last hair. He was very blond. I shall not say that his appearance was vulgar, but it was altogether commonplace; and he might have spared himself all his pains, for his impeccably cut clothes sat upon him, not as his own, but as his tailor's. Even that well-set-up head and those hands, so well turned and smooth, looked as if they had been attached out of the living flesh to his collar or his sleeves, and might without any detriment have been exhibited as amputated waxwork objects in a hairdresser's or glove-maker's window. To hear him talk, to watch him bat his sky-blue-enamel eyes, to the accompaniment of a perennially blissful smile for everything that issued from his own coraline lips, and then to see him open his eyes again, the right lid remaining a little drawn and gummed there, as if he could not quite succeed in tearing himself away so abruptly from the sumptuous relish of an inner satisfaction that none would have supposed was in him—all this could not but make the strangest sort of impression, so artificial did it all seem; I repeat: a tailor's dummy and a barber's head.

And now, expecting to see him like this, the surprise of finding him all disheveled and perturbed only served to arouse in me, upon the spur of the moment, a desire to experience that exquisite feeling of risk with which one sets out, unarmed and smiling, against an armed enemy who threatens, after having intimated to the adversary that he is not to stir a step. My mood having been rekindled in me, it left upon my lips a disdainful smile and an obliviousness upon my brow, as I thought of the game that was to follow, a highly perilous one in view of the grave interests at stake, for this man and all the others: the fate of the bank; the fate of my family; I was to have yet further proof of the terrible thing I already knew, namely, that I should inevitably appear more mad than ever now, with the speeches which I was preparing to make, being headed at breakneck speed down the incline of that incredible, unlikely-seeming *ingenuousness* which had so amazed Quantorzo, and which had caused my wife to burst her sides with laughing.

The truth was that, even for myself from now on, if I looked at things squarely, that point of conscience to which I strove to cling could no longer serve me as a valid excuse. Did I in all seriousness feel any sting in the reproach of a usuriousness which I in intent had never practised? I had, it was true, given the bank my signature as a formality; I had lived, up to this moment, upon the bank's earnings, without ever having given the matter a thought; but now that at last I had stopped to think of it, I would withdraw my money from the bank and at once, by way of putting myself wholly right, should be free of it all by founding a work of charity or something of the sort.

"What! And you think it's nothing, all that! Good God, so it's true then, is it?"

"What's true?"

"That you have gone mad! And my daughter, what is going to become of her? How do you expect to live? On what?"

"Ah, that's just it; that is rather important, as I see it. Something to be studied out."

"You would ruin yourself forever, would you? Why, everyone has always looked after his own affairs, since time began."

"That is very good. And from this time forth, I am going to look after mine."

"But how are you looking after them, if you throw away the money that your father made with all those years of labor?"

"I have had six years in the University."

"Ah! Do you expect to go back to the University?"

"I might."

He made a gesture as if to rise. I restrained him.

"Excuse me," I said, "but I suppose it will take some little time to liquidate the bank's affairs?"

"What are you talking about! Liquidation! Liquidation! Liquidation!"

"If you don't care to hear what I have to say—"

He whirled on me.

"You're raving!"

"I am very calm," I observed. "I was about to remark that there are so many courses which I had carried to a certain point and then dropped."

He gave me an astonished stare.

"Courses? What do you mean?"

"That I might, in short order, take a degree in medicine, for example, or become a doctor of letters and philosophy."

"You?"

"You don't believe it? It's true. I started studying medicine. Had three years of it. And I liked it. Just ask Dida which she'd rather see her Gengè be. A doctor or a professor. I have a ready tongue; I might even, if I liked, be a lawyer."

He shook himself violently:

"Seeing that you've never cared to do anything up to now!"

"That's true enough. But it has not been due to frivolity, you know. I went into things too deeply. And believe me, you will never succeed by going too deeply into anything whatsoever. Supposing you should happen to make certain discoveries! But I can assure you that, in a superficial fashion, I could very well be a doctor, a lawyer, or a professor, as Dida may prefer. All I have to do is to apply myself."

Purple in the face from the violent effect that my words produced upon him, he at this point ran out, or rather, burst out of the room. I ran after him.

"Just think," I shouted at his retreating figure, "how popular I shall be by giving my father's money away! I might even be elected deputy, think of that! If Dida liked it, and you too—a deputy for a son-in-law—can't you just see me! Can't you just see me!"

But he had already fled, screaming at my every word:

"Madman! Madman! Madman!"

V

I Say, Why Not?

MY TONE, I do not deny, was a jesting one, owing to that devilish mood of mine. It well may seem, I realize, that my conversation was fatuous in the extreme. Yet my remarks concerning Gengè's becoming a doctor or a lawyer or a professor, or even a deputy, while they might make me smile, ought still, I insist, to have compelled in him at least that respect and consideration which in the provinces are commonly shown to those worthy professions, so frequently practiced by mediocrities, with whom it would not have been at all difficult for me to compete.

The explanation, as I well know, was a different one. It was that he, my father-in-law, *could not see me in any one of them.* For reasons quite different from my own. He could not countenance my taking his son-in-law (that Gengè of heaven knows what sort that he saw in me) out of the conditions under which the latter had lived up to then, that is to say, my destroying that comfortable marionette-like consistency which he on the one hand and his daughter on the other, and all my associates of the bank for their part, had attributed to him. I must leave him as he was, that "good lad but wild" of a Gengè, to live on without taking any thought of the usurious practices of a bank that was not managed by himself.

And I swear that I would have left him there, in order not to disturb that poor little doll of mine, whose love was so very, very dear to me, and in order not to occasion so grave a turmoil for so many good folk who wished me well, if, by so leaving him for others, I might on my own account have gone elsewhere, with another body and another name.

VI

Stifling a Laugh

I KNEW, moreover, that by placing myself under new conditions of life, by appearing to others tomorrow as a doctor, let us say, or a lawyer, or a professor, I should no more than before have found myself either one to all or an individual to myself, as I went about in the garb and performing the functions of any one of those professions. Everything was now comprised in the horror of being locked within the prison of any form whatsoever.

None the less, those remarks which I had laughingly made to my father-in-law were the same ones that I had made in all seriousness to myself the whole night long, as I stifled the laugh provoked by a mental picture of myself as a lawyer, or a doctor, or a professor. I had, in short, reflected that I might, as a matter of necessity, have accepted and taken up any one of those professions, or any other, had Dida, coming back to me as I desired, laid upon me the obligation of providing in the best way I could for her new manner of life with a new Gengè. From my father-in-law's impetuous exit, however, I could argue that, even for Dida, no new Gengè could be born of the old. The latter was merely making it plain to her that he was hopelessly mad, by thus desiring at a moment's notice and *for no reason at all*, to rid himself of those conditions under which he had lived happily up to then.

And I must have been mad, indeed, to expect a doll-like thing such as she to go mad along with me like this, *for no reason at all*.

BOOK SEVENTH

BOOK SEVENTH

I

Complications

I RECEIVED a note delivered by hand the next morning, inviting me to come at once to the house of Anna Rosa, my wife's woman friend, whom I have mentioned once or twice in passing at the beginning of this narrative.

I was expecting that someone would seek to intervene, by way of attempting a reconciliation between myself and Dida; but this someone, I supposed, would come from my father-in-law and my associates at the bank, rather than directly from my wife, especially seeing that the sole obstacle to be removed was my intention of liquidating the bank. Between my wife and myself, practically nothing had happened. All I should have to do would be to assure Anna Rosa that I was sincerely repentant for my rudeness to Dida, for having shaken her and thrown her down upon a chair—I had merely to say this, and the reconciliation would be effected without further ado. That Anna Rosa should take upon herself the burden of persuading me to give up my intention, making this a stipulation for my wife's return home, did not impress me as being in any manner a tenable assumption.

Dida had told me that her friend had declined, out of contempt for money, a number of so-termed advantageous offers of marriage, bringing down upon herself thereby the reprobation of all sensible folk, and even of Dida, who in marrying me (I mean, a usurer's son), must certainly have given her women friends to understand that she was doing it for the reason that, when all was said and done, it was an "advantageous" match. And accordingly, when it came to saving that "advantage" now, Anna Rosa was not the most apt spokesman.

The contrary was rather to be assumed, that Dida had had recourse to her aid in getting word to me that her father, acting in agreement with my other associates, was restraining her in his house and preventing her coming back to me, unless I gave up my intention of liquidating the bank. Knowing my wife as I did, however, this did not appear to me any more tenable a conclusion than the other.

It was, therefore, with a consuming curiosity that I went to keep this appointment, the reason for which I could not succeed in guessing.

II

First Inkling

I KNEW Anna Rosa very slightly. I had seen her a number of times at my house, but having always kept my distance, more by instinct than as a result of deliberation, from my wife's women friends, I had exchanged very few words with her. A certain faint smile which I had surprised upon her lips now and then, as she gave me a fugitive glance, had seemed to me so obviously inspired by that silly image of me to which my wife Dida's Gengè had given birth in her mind that I had never thought it might be amusing to talk to her.

I had never been at her home.

An orphan on both sides, she lived with an aged aunt in a house which looked as if it had been jammed up against the very high walls of the Badía Grande, the walls of an old castle, through the curved iron-grated windows of which, looking out over the sunset, could be glimpsed the faces of the handful of elderly Sisters that were left there. One of these Sisters, the youngest of them all, was at the same time Anna Rosa's paternal aunt; and she was, it was said, half-mad. But it does not take a great deal to drive a woman mad, when she is shut up in a nunnery. From my wife, who had been at school for three years in the convent of San Vincenzo, I had learned that all the Sisters, old and young, were a little mad in one way or another.

I did not find Anna Rosa at home. The old servant who took the note from my hand, speaking to me mysteriously through a slit without opening the door, informed me that her young mistress was up in the Abbey, with her aunt, the nun, and that I might go look for her there; she told me to ask the one who opened the door to show me into Sister Celestina's parlor. All this mystery amazed me; and I at first, by way of heightening my curiosity, held myself back from going. I felt the need of first reflecting, in so far as was possible in the stupor I was in, upon the strangeness of that appointment up there in the Abbey, in a Sister's little parlor.

Any link between my futile marital misadventure and this invitation seemed now to have been broken, and a feeling of apprehension swiftly came over me, as at an unforeseen complication that would entail who could say what consequences for my future life. As everyone at Richieri knows, it came near entailing my death. But here, I should like to repeat what I told the judges, in order that I may blot out once and forever, from the minds of all, the suspicion that my deposition was made at the time with the object of saving Anna Rosa and absolving her from any blame. There was no blame on her part. The blame must fall upon me, or rather, upon my previous tortured train of thought, if the unlooked-for and undreamed-of adventure into which, almost without willing it, I let myself be drawn for one last desperate experiment came near to having such an end as this.

III

The Revolver Among the Flowers

By ONE of those little slippery side-streets of the old
town of Richieri which during the day are infected
with the stench of rotting garbage, I made my way
up to the Abbey.

When one has formed the habit of living in a certain manner, there is a sort of indescribable pertur-
bation connected with going to a silent and unac-
customed place, with the suspicion that there is
something there present which for us is shrouded
in mystery, a mystery from which our spirit is condemned to keep its distance; the thought comes to
us that, if we enter there, our whole life possibly
will open up in nameless new sensations, and we
shall feel that we are living in another world.

That Abbey, an old feudal castle of the Cler-
monts, with its low entrance door all worm-eaten,
and the huge courtyard with the basin in the middle,
that worn, darkly echoing great stair with the feel
of a grotto, that long, wide corridor with all the
doors opening off it on either side, and the red bricks
of the crumbling pavement, gleaming in the light
from the high window at the further end, which
opened upon a skyey silence—how many vicissitudes and changing aspects of life had it witnessed
in passing and gathered to itself? And now, as that
handful of Sisters wandered about like lost souls

within it and waited for a death that was slow in coming, it appeared no longer to possess any consciousness of itself. All there within was forgetfulness, as those last Sisters waited one by one, a long, long wait for the end; the very purpose for which this baronial pile had originally been thrown up, and how it had come to be for so many centuries an abbey—all was long since buried in oblivion.

A Sister opened one of those doors off the corridor and led me into the little parlor. A bell down below had already rung with a melancholy sound; perhaps, it was to summon Sister Celestina. The parlor was so dark that at first I could not make out anything other than the grating at the far end, barely visible by the light that came in when the door was opened. I stood there waiting; and I cannot say how long I might have remained standing like that, if a feeble voice from the grating had not finally invited me to seat myself, adding that Anna Rosa would be up from the convent garden.

I shall not attempt to convey the impression which that unexpected voice in the darkness, from the other side of the grating, produced upon me. There shone for me in that darkness the sun which must be shining in the Abbey garden; I did not know where the garden was, but it must be very, very green; and then, of a sudden, in the midst of all that green, there was a flood of light revealing the person of Anna Rosa, as I never before had beheld it, all a-tremble with a mischievous loveliness. It was a flash. The dark came back. Or rather, not the dark, because I could now make out the grating and, in front of it, a small table and a couple of chairs. The grating was wrapped in silence. I sought the voice, feeble but fresh-sounding, almost youthful, that had spoken to me. There was no one there any more. And yet, it must have been the voice of an old woman. Anna Rosa, that voice, this little parlor, the sun in that darkness, the green of the garden—my head was fairly swimming.

Shortly afterward, Anna Rosa hastily opened the door and called me out of the little parlor into the corridor. She was very flushed, her hair was disordered, her eyes were sparkling, her white knit woolen chemisette was unbuttoned over her bosom, as if she were too warm, and in her arms she had ever so many flowers and a long runner of ivy that protruded from behind, under one shoulder. Inviting me to follow her, she ran down to the end of the corridor and started up the little stair under the window. It was as she went to climb the stairs; it may be that she had put up her hand to keep a part of her flowers from falling; in any case, what she did let fall from her other hand was her purse; and instantly, there was the sound of a shot, followed by a piercing scream that echoed down the length of the corridor.

I was barely in time to support Anna Rosa, who fell back upon me. In my amazement, before I could succeed in making out what had happened, I saw about me seven aged Sisters, peering at me with a terrified gaze. At the sound of the shot, they had come running out into the corridor; and catching sight of me there with Anna Rosa wounded in my arms, they had been seized by a consternation which I at first was at a loss to understand, so impossible did it seem to me that they should not be possessed by the same concern as myself, as I shouted out to them to find a bed on which we could lay the wounded woman. Their answer was, "Monsignor"; Monsignor was expected at any minute. And Anna Rosa, as she lay in my arms, cried, "The revolver! The revolver!" She wanted me, that is, to retrieve for her the revolver that was in her purse, because it was a keepsake of her father.

That in the fallen purse there must be a revolver which, by going off, had wounded her in the foot, was at once evident to me, but not the reason for which she carried it with her, especially on the morning when she had had an appointment with me at the Abbey. It impressed me as being very strange; but at the moment, it did not so much as remotely enter my mind that she might have carried it for me. More than ever astonished by it all, and perceiving that no one was lending me any aid in caring for the victim, I took the latter bodily in my arms and bore her out of the Abbey, down the little side-street, to her home.

I had to make my way back up to the Abbey a little later, to pick up from the floor of the corridor, under the high window, that revolver which was to be used on me.

IV

The Explanation

THE news of the strange accident which had happened at the Badía Grande, and of how I had rushed out carrying the wounded Anna Rosa in my arms, spread through Richieri in a flash, at once occasioning malicious exaggerations which by reason of their absurdity appeared to me at first utterly ridiculous. I was far from supposing that they might not only sound likely, but even be accepted as the unqualified truth, not alone by those to whose interest it was to stir the thing up and keep it going, but even by the wounded one whom I carried in my arms.

That is exactly the way it was.

For Gengè, my good people, my wife Dida's dreadfully stupid Gengè, was cherishing, without my knowing anything about it, an ardent feeling for Anna Rosa. It was Dida who had put it into her head; for it was Dida who had noticed it. She had never said anything about it to Gengè, but had confided it with a smile to her friend, to give the latter pleasure and also possibly by way of explaining to her what Gengè's motive for shunning her was, when she came to call: it was the fear of falling in love with her. I do not feel that I have any right to deny this feeling of Gengè's toward Anna Rosa. The most I can do is to maintain that it was not

227

true so far as I was concerned; and yet, even this is not accurate, seeing that the fact of the matter is, I never had taken the trouble to find out whether it was sympathy or antipathy that I felt toward this friend of my wife. I think I have already sufficiently established the point that Gengè's reality did not belong to me, but to my wife, Dida, who had conferred it upon him.

If Dida, then, attributed to her Gengè this secret attraction, it made little difference whether or not it was true for me; it was so very true for her that she found in it my reason for keeping my distance from Anna Rosa; and it was so true for Anna that the fugitive glances which I from time to time had cast in her direction had been interpreted by her as something more; I was no longer that darling little silly of a Gengè that my wife imagined me to be, but a most unhappy Signor Gengè, who must be suffering untold physical tortures at being thus esteemed and loved by his own wife.

For, come to think of it, a thing of this sort is the least of the consequences that may follow from all the unsuspected realities that others attribute to us. Superficially, we are in the habit of calling such things as this, false suppositions, erroneous judgments, gratuitous attributions. Yet everything that may be imagined of us is really possible, even though it may not be true for us. True for us? Others laugh. It is true for them. So true is it, understand, that if you do not hold fast to that reality which is bestowed upon you as your own, they are in a position to bring you to realize that the reality which they confer upon you is truer than any of your own. No one has a better right to speak from experience than I.

I found myself, then, knowing nothing at all about it, very much in love with Anna Rosa, and for this reason, involved in the accidental shooting at the Abbey, a thing which I should never, never have imagined. As I waited upon Anna Rosa, after having carried her home in my arms, placed her upon her bed, run for a doctor and a nurse and given her such domestic first-aid as was possible, I was not long in becoming aware, myself, that it was both possible and true, what she had fancied of me as a result of Dida's confidences, that is, my feeling toward her. And I was to have all the explanations, as I sat there at the foot of her bed, in the rose-hued intimacy of her little room, which was marred by an unpleasant medicinal odor.

She laughed heartily at the idea that anyone could imagine she had carried that weapon for me, in giving me an appointment at the Abbey! That little revolver was a thing that she carried with her always, in her purse; she had so carried it ever since the day she had found it, in the pocket of a waistcoat belonging to her father, who had died suddenly six years before. Very small, with a mother-of-pearl handle and brightly gleaming all over, it had struck her fancy as a trinket that was all the more to be cherished for the reason that a death-dealing potency lay concealed in its pretty barrel. More than once, she confided to me, upon those occasions by no means rare when, owing to certain strange soul-fears, the world round about her had impressed her as being terrifyingly empty, she had been tempted to make use of it, and had run her fingers with a sensuous delight over the smooth, gleaming steel and the mother-of-pearl. But now that it, in place of being pointed deliberately at her temple or her heart, had displayed the power to *wound her* accidentally in her foot, at the risk—as she feared— of leaving her a cripple for life, she experienced a strange displeasure. She felt that she had so appropriated it that it ought not any longer to possess any such power over her. She saw it now as a *naughty* thing. Taking it out of the drawer of the commode at the head of her bed, she looked it over and repeated: "Naughty!"

But that appointment up there in the Abbey, in the little parlor of her aunt, the nun—what was the meaning of that? And those Sisters who, instead of thinking of her when she was wounded, kept on talking to me, as if obsessed by the idea, of the visit of some Monsignor—or other?

I was to have the explanation of this mystery, also.

She had known that Monsignor Partanna, Bishop of Richieri, was due to pay a visit that morning, as was his monthly custom, to the aged Sisters of the Badía Grande. For the Sisters, this visit was as a foretaste of heavenly bliss; and to risk having it spoiled by an accident of that sort would have been for them the most untoward of circumstances. And she had sent for me to come to the Abbey for the reason that she wished me to have a talk at once, that very morning, with the Bishop.

"I have a talk with the Bishop? Why?"

To frustrate in time the plots that were afoot against me.

They wished, as a matter of fact, to have me declared of unsound mind and to have a guardian appointed for me. Dida had informed her that they had already got together in legal form all the evidence, Firbo's, Quantorzo's, her father's, her own, by way of establishing my flagrant lack of mental balance. There were any number who were ready to give their testimony, even to that fellow Turolla, whose part I had taken against Firbo and all the other employees of the bank—even to Marco di Dio, to whom I had made the donation of a house.

"But," I could not refrain from observing to Anna Rosa, "he will lose it. If I am declared of unsound mind, the donation will be null and void."

Anna Rosa burst out laughing in my face at this ingenuous remark. They had promised Marco di Dio that. if he testified as they desired, he would not lose the house. And what was more, he was in a position to testify in all good conscience.

I glanced suspiciously at the laughing Anna Rosa. She noticed it.

"Why, of course!" she cried. "It was all quite mad! Quite mad! Quite mad!"

Not only that, she enjoyed it all; she approved it; and more than ever, if I really meant to go through with it and commit the supreme folly of ruining the bank and dismissing a woman who had always been my enemy.

"Dida?"

"You don't believe it?"

"Yes, an enemy now."

"No, always! always!"

And she went on to tell me how, for some time past, she had endeavored to bring my wife to see that I was not the silly fellow she imagined me to be; they had had long talks on the subject, and she, Anna Rosa, had been at infinite pains to curb the contempt she felt at that woman's obstinate determination to see in all my words and actions either a silliness that was not there or an evil intent such as only a deliberately hostile mind could possibly have discovered in them.

I was thunderstruck. As by a lightning flash, these confidences of Anna Rosa's afforded me a glimpse of a Dida so different from my own, and yet so equally true, that I experienced—at this point more than ever—the full horror of that discovery which I had made. A Dida who spoke of me as I absolutely never should have imagined she could speak, an enemy of my very flesh. To have all the intimate memories that we shared so unworthily torn asunder and betrayed that I could bring myself to think of them only by summoning up my contempt for an element of the ridiculous in them of which I had not before been aware, and by falling back upon a sense of shame which previously, in my heart of hearts, it had not seemed to me that I was bound to feel. It was as if, after having treacherously induced me in all confidence to lay bare my soul, she had thrown wide the door, exposing me to the derision of anyone who cared to enter and behold me thus nude and with nowhere to hide. Appraisals of my family, and judgments passed upon the most natural of my habits, such as I should never have expected of her. In short, another Dida; a Dida who was, in all truth, an enemy.

And yet, I am as certain as certain can be that, with her Gengè, she was not pretending; she was, with her Gengè, what she was capable of being to him, perfectly whole-hearted and sincere. Away from the life she led with him, she became another person, that other person that she found it convenient to be, that she preferred being, or that she really felt herself to be to Anna Rosa.

But what occasion for wonderment did I find in this? Could I not leave her Gengè intact for her, as she had fashioned him, and go on being another person on my own account?

It was with me as it is with all.

I must not reveal the secret of my discovery to Anna Rosa. She herself had tempted me to do so, by the surprising things she had told me about my wife. And I never should have imagined that this revelation would be able to produce in me the spiritual turmoil that it did produce, to the point of leading me to commit that mad act which I did commit.

But I shall first tell of my visit to Monsignor, a step which she herself urged upon me with great insistency, as a thing that could not be put off any longer.

V

The God Within and the God Without

IN THE days when I used to take Bibi, my wife's bitch, out walking, the churches of Richieri were my despair. Come what might, Bibi was bent upon entering them. When I called her back, she would rise up on her haunches, shake one of her front paws and sneeze; and then, with one ear up and the other down, she would sit there gazing at me as if she could not believe it possible—no, it was not possible—that a pretty little she-dog like herself should not be permitted to enter a church. Especially, seeing that there was no one there!

"No one? What do you mean, no one, Bibi?" I would say to her. "There is the most respectable of human sentiments there. You cannot understand these things, because, as luck will have it, you are a she-dog and not a man. Men—do you understand?—have need of building a house even for their sentiments. It is not enough for them to have those sentiments within them, in their hearts; they want to see them outside, as well, so that they can touch them; and so, they proceed to build them a house."

For me, it had always been enough up to then to have within me, after my own fashion, the sentiment of God. Out of respect to the one that others had, I always had restrained Bibi from entering a

234

church; but I did not enter, either. I kept my own sentiment and strove to live up to it, by remaining erect on my feet instead of going to kneel in a house which others had built for Him. That *quick* which had been stabbed in me, when my wife had laughed at hearing me say that I did not care any longer to have myself looked upon as a usurer at Richieri, was undoubtedly God: God, who had been wounded in me, God who in me could no longer bear that others at Richieri should look upon me as a usurer. But had I gone to say a thing like this to Quantorzo or to Firbo and my other associates of the bank, I should certainly only have been furnishing them with a further proof of my madness.

And now it was necessary for this God within, this God who in me would have seemed mad to all, to go as contritely as possible to pay a call upon and to ask aid and protection of the all-wise God without, who possessed his own house, his most faithful and jealous servants, and all those wisely and magnificently constituted powers that caused him to be loved and feared in the world.

At this God, there was no danger that Firbo or Quantorzo would dare to fling the taunt of madness.

VI

An Inconvenient Bishop

I MADE my way then to the Episcopal Residence to pay my respects to Monsignor Partanna.

It was a matter of talk at Richieri that Monsignor had been elected Bishop at the instance and thanks to the shady offices of powerful prelates at Rome. The fact was that, although he had been at the head of the diocese for a number of years, he had not succeeded in ingratiating himself or in winning either the sympathy or the confidence of a single soul.

At Richieri, the townspeople had grown used to the pomp, the jovial and cordial manners and the bounteous munificence of the Bishop's late predecessor, the Most Excellent Monsignor Vivaldi; and it was accordingly with a tug at their heartstrings that they had beheld for the first time, coming down on foot from the Episcopal Palace, the great-coated skeleton-like figure of the new Bishop, accompanied by his two secretaries. A Bishop on foot? Ever since the Episcopal Mansion had been perched up there, like a lowering fortress above the city, the Bishops had always come down in a handsome two-horse carriage with red crests and trimmings.

Monsignor Partanna, on the other hand, had let it be understood upon taking his seat that he looked upon the episcopacy as a charge and not as a worldly honor. He had dismissed servants and cook, coachman and footmen, had given up his carriage, and had inaugurated the strictest economy, all this in spite of the fact that the diocese of Richieri was among the wealthiest in Italy. For his pastoral diocesan visits, a custom which had been permitted very largely to lapse by his predecessor, but one which he observed with the utmost vigilance at the canonical seasons, notwithstanding the very bad condition of the roads and the lack of means of transportation, he made use of hired carriages or even of asses and of mules.

I had, moreover, learned from Anna Rosa that all the Sisters of the five monasteries in the city, with the exception of the decrepit ones in the Badia Grande, hated him for the heartless regulations which, immediately upon becoming Bishop, he had enacted for their discipline, regulations to the effect that they were no longer to manufacture or to sell comfits or rosolio, those delicious comfits made of honey and real pastry and done up with ribbons and silver cord, and that delicious rosolio, which tasted of anise and of cinnamon! They were not to embroider any more, not even altar cloths or vestments, but were to devote their attention solely to knitting; and lastly, they were not to be permitted to keep their private confessors, but were to make use, all of them without distinction, of the communal Padre. And he had gone on to lay down yet more arduous rules for the canons and beneficials of all the churches, demanding, in short, the most rigid observance of every duty on the part of all ecclesiastics.

A Bishop such as this is not a convenient one for all those who would externalize their sentiment of God, by building for the deity an outside house, all the more handsome as the need for pardon is greater. But for me, he was the best I could possibly have had. His predecessor, the Most Excellent Monsignor Vivaldi, who was on good terms with and knew how to handle everybody, would undoubtedly have looked for the ways and means of patching everything up, by saving at once my conscience and the bank, in such a manner as to satisfy me and, at the same time, Firbo and Quantorzo and all the rest.

But I now felt that I could no longer patch things up, either with myself or with anyone.

VII

An Interview With Monsignor

MONSIGNOR PARTANNA received me in the huge old chancery hall of the Episcopal Palace. My nostrils are still conscious of the odor of that hall, with its gloomy ceiling, the frescoes of which were so dust-covered as to be scarcely longer distinguishable. The high walls with their yellowing plaster were incumbered with ancient portraits of prelates, which were likewise stained with dust and some of them with mould as well, being hung up here and there with no sort of order, over the cabinets and the faded worm-eaten bookcases.

At the farther end of the hall were two great windows, the panes of which, affording an indescribably melancholy view of a racuous stretch of overcast sky, were being incessantly shaken by the strong wind which had suddenly come up, the terrible Richieri wind, which brings anxiety into every house. It seemed at times as if those panes must give way before the howling fury of the southwester. My whole conversation with Monsignor was to the sinister accompaniment of shrill and vehement hissings and dark-boding long-drawn-out shrieks which, frequently taking my mind off the Monsignor's words, made me feel, with an indefinable dismay such as I never before had known, the grievous vanity of time and of human life.

I recall that, through one of those windows, I

caught sight of the small terrace of an old house opposite. Upon that terrace there appeared without warning a man who must have just got out of bed with the insane idea of experiencing the voluptuousness of flight. Exposed there to the fury of the wind, he was holding up so that it might flap about his thin body, so thin that it sent a shudder down one's spine, his red woolen bedcoverlet, suspended from and supported by his arms which were crossed under his shoulders. And all the while, he was laughing— laughing with a glint of tears in his bedeviled eyes, while his long reddish locks of hair flew about him, to this side and that, like licking tongues of flame.

This apparition so stupefied me that, after a certain time, I was unable to refrain from calling it to Monsignor's attention, thereby interrupting a highly serious sermon upon conscientious scruples, a sermon upon which the Bishop had launched forth some while back, finding an evident satisfaction in his own reasoning powers. Monsignor turned and barely glanced out the window, then gave one of those smiles which are so excellent a substitute for a sigh.

"Ah, yes," he said, "it is a poor madman who lives over there."

He said it with such a tone of indifference, as one speaks of something to which one's eyes have long since become accustomed, that I was tempted to startle him by declaring: "No, he doesn't live over there at all. He lives here, Monsignor. That madman who wants to fly is myself." I held myself in, however, and did not say it. I put on instead a similar air of indifference.

"And is there no danger," I asked, "of his falling off the terrace?"

"No," was Monsignor's reply, "he's been like that for a good many years. Harmless. Quite harmless."

Spontaneously, indeed without any will of my own, the words burst from me then:

"Like me."

Monsignor could not but be startled at this. But I quickly put on so placid and smiling a countenance that everything was at once remedied. I hastened to explain that I meant that I was similarly harmless in the minds of Signor Firbo and Signor Quantorzo and my father-in-law and my wife—all of those, in brief, who wished to restrain my actions. Monsignor, once more serene, resumed his sermon upon conscientious scruples, one that he deemed particularly appropriate in my case, this being the only manner in which he might cause his authority, his prestige and spiritual power, to prevail over the schemings and manoeuvrings of those enemies of mine.

Was I to give him to understand that mine was not precisely such a case of conscience as he imagined? Had I dared tell him this, I should at once have become mad in his eyes, too. The God in me, who wanted to take my money out of the bank in order that I might no longer be called a usurer, was a God who was an enemy to all buildings. That God, on the contrary, to whom I had come for aid and protection was nothing if not a builder. He would, it was true, lend me a hand in getting my money out of the bank, but on condition that I made use of it in building a house to another of the most respectable of human sentiments: charity.

Monsignor, at the end of our interview, asked me with a solemn air if this was not what I meant to do. I had to tell him that it was. He thereupon rang an old, tarnished, faint-sounding little bell that stood very shyly upon the table. A young cleric, blond and extremely pale, appeared. Monsignor ordered him to go summon Don Antonio Sclepis, a canon of the Cathedral and superintendent of the College of Oblates, who was in the anteroom. He was the very man for me.

I knew this priest by reputation rather than personally. I had gone once, on my father's behalf, to deliver a letter to him, up to the College of Oblates, which stands not far from the Episcopal Palace at the highest point of the city, being a huge and very ancient edifice, square-built and darkly lowering without, all weather-beaten and time-worn, but all white, airy and flooded with light on the inside. It is here that the poor orphans and the little bastards from all over the province are taken in, from the age of six to eighteen, and it is here that they are taught the various arts and crafts. The discipline of the place is so severe that when those poor Oblates sing matins or vespers, to the sound of the organ in the Collegiate church, their prayers, as heard from down below, are as heart-rending as a prisoners' lament.

To judge from his appearance, one would not have thought that the Canon Sclepis had in him so much strength, energy and power of will. He was a tall, spare priest, almost transparent; it was as if all the light and air of the perch where he lived not only had faded but had also rarefied him, giving to his hands a quivering slenderness, while the lids of his bright oval-shaped eyes were thinner than an onion-peel. His voice, also, was colorless and quavering, and there was an empty smile on his broad white lips, which frequently exuded a few drops of saliva.

No sooner had he come in and been informed by Monsignor of my conscientious scruples and my intentions, than he at once began talking to me, in great haste and with great confidence, clapping a hand upon my shoulder and addressing me by the familiar *tu:*

"That is very good, my son. A great sorrow pleases me. Thank God for it. Sorrow shall be your salvation, my son. One must be stern with all the foolish ones who have not the will to suffer. But it has been your fortune to suffer greatly, thinking of your father who, poor man, eh? did so very much evil! Let this be your sackcloth, the thought of your father! Your sackcloth! And leave it to me to fight it out with Signor Firbo and Signor Quantorzo! They want to stop you, do they? I'll take care of them for you, have no fear of that!"

I left the Episcopal Palace feeling certain that I had as good as won out over those who were trying to take affairs out of my hands; but this certainty and the obligations that went with it, which I had just now contracted with the Bishop and with Sclepis, cast me into a boundless sea of uncertainty as to what was to become of me, when I should be deprived of all, with no longer any status or a family.

VIII

Waiting

I HAD nothing left to think of for the moment except Anna Rosa, who wished me to keep her company while she was confined with her wounded foot. She stayed in bed with her foot in a bandage; and she vowed that she would never get up again, if, as the doctors still feared, she was to remain a cripple. Her pallor and her languor from her long disability had conferred upon her a fresh loveliness in place of the old. The light in her eyes was more intense, almost saturnine. She informed me that she was unable to sleep. The scent from her thick black hair, a little inclined to be crisp and curly, when she found it of a morning all undone and strewn over her pillow, suffocated her. Had it not been that she could not bear a hairdresser's hands upon her head, she would have had it shorn. She asked me one morning if I could not shear it for her. She laughed at my embarrassment in replying to this question, and then drew the sheet up over her face and remained that way for a long time, in silence and with her face hidden.

Under the bed-coverings, the shapeliness of her body, which was that of a mature virgin, was tantalizingly visible. I knew from Dida that she was twenty-five years of age. As she lay thus with her face hidden, the thought must have occurred to her that I could do no less than stare at the outlines of her body under the sheets. She was tempting me. In the semi-darkness of the disordered little rose-hued bedroom, the very silence seemed conscious of the vain expectancy of a life which the momentary whims of that weird creature would never be able to bring to any sort of fruition, to which they would never be able to give any sort of consistency.

I had divined in her an absolute intolerance for anything that showed signs of lasting or assuming stability. Everything she did, every desire that sprang up in her, every thought that occurred to her at one moment, a moment later was ever so far removed from her; and if she felt herself still drawn by anything in the past, this was followed by outbursts of anger and fits of maniacal rage, a complete emotional upset.

Her body alone, it appeared, gave her a never-failing pleasure, although at times she exhibited anything but satisfaction with it, and even asserted that she hated it. Nevertheless, she was constantly surveying it in the mirror, in its every part and feature, trying out every conceivable pose, every expression of which her intently gleaming and vivacious eyes, her trembling nostrils, her red, disdainful mouth and her exceedingly mobile lower jaw were capable. This was due, rather, to the actress in her; it was not because she fancied that in life they could be of any use to her except as a game, a momentary game of coquetry and flirtatiousness.

One morning, I caught sight of her trying on and studying intently in a small hand-mirror, which she always kept in bed with her, a tender and compassionate smile; yet her eyes all the while gleamed with an almost childish mischievousness. And then, to see her do over that same smile for me, to see it live upon her lips as if it had sprung up there just now, spontaneously, for me—all this provoked in me an impulse to rebellion. I informed her that I was not her mirror. She was not offended, however, but asked me if that smile which I had just beheld was the same one that she had seen and been studying in the looking-glass.

"What do you expect me to know about it? I am not by any means in a position to know how you look to yourself. You ought to have your photograph taken with that smile."

"I have had," she said. "A big one. It's there in the drawer of that clothespress. Get it out, please."

That drawer was full of photographs of her. She showed me any number, old and recent.

"All dead," I told her.

She turned her head and glanced at me quickly: "Dead?"

"Yes, for all they appear to be alive."

"Even this one with the smile?"

"Yes. And this pensive one; and the one with the eyes drooped."

"But how can they be dead, if I here am alive?"

"Ah, you, yes; because you do not see yourself now. But when you are in front of a mirror, the moment you look at yourself again, you are no longer alive."

"And why not?"

"Because, in order to behold yourself, you must for a moment halt life within you. Excuse me, but seeing that you go to the photographer's so often— when the photographer, in front of you with his camera, tells you to be sure not to move, you must have noticed—life is suspended in you—and you feel that such suspension cannot last more than a second—it is like turning into a statue— For life is constant motion, and one can never really see one's self."

"You mean to say that I, while living, have never seen myself?"

"Never; not as I can see you. But I see a likeness of you that is mine and mine alone; it is assuredly not yours. You, while living, have possibly been able to catch no more than a bare glimpse of your own in some snapshot or other that has been made of you; and it has come as an unpleasant surprise; it may even have pained you to recognize yourself, in helter-skelter motion like that."

"That's true."

"For you can only know yourself when you strike an attitude: a statue: not alive. When one is alive, one lives and does not see himself. To know one's self is to die. The reason you spend so much time looking at yourself in that mirror, in all mirrors, is that you are not alive; you do not know how to live, you cannot or you do not want to live. You want too much to know yourself; and meanwhile, you are not living."

"Why, nothing of the sort! I never can succeed in keeping still a moment."

"But you want to see yourself always. In every act of your life. It is as if you had before you always the likeness of yourself, in every action, in every gesture. It is from this that your intolerance comes. You do not want the feeling in you to be blind. You compel it to open its eyes and look at itself in a mirror which you are forever holding up in front of it. And feeling, the moment it sees itself, turns ice within you. You cannot go on living before a mirror. One's aim should be never to see one's self. For the reason that, however much you may try, you can never know yourself as others see you. And of what use is it, then, to know one's self for one's self's sake? You may even come to the point where you will no longer be able to understand why you must have that likeness which the mirror gives you back."

She remained for long, staring straight ahead of her, lost in thought. I am certain that, after this speech of mine, after I had told her of all my spiritual torment, there yawned before us, for her as for me, at this moment, the boundless and terrifyingly bright vision of the irremediable solitude that was ours. Every object in appearance took on a dread-inspiring isolation. And it may be that she no longer saw the reason for bearing about with her that face, if in that solitude not even she would be able to see herself alive, while others from without, isolating her at their will, would go on seeing her Heaven only knew how.

All pride fell.

To see things with eyes that could not know how others all the while saw them.

To speak and not to be understood.

It was no longer worth anything to be something for one's self.

And nothing was any longer true, if nothing was true, for itself. Each one on his own account assumed it to be so and appropriated it to himself, by way of filling up as best he might his own solitude and conferring some sort of consistency, from day to day, upon his own life.

I stood there at the foot of her bed, with an aspect that was to me unknown and to her unfathomable, a castaway in her solitude and she in mine, as she lay there before me upon her bed, with her motionless and far-away eyes, pale-faced and with an elbow on her pillow, her head supported by her hand. She felt invincibly attracted by all that I had said; and at the same time, it gave her a sort of shudder, at times almost a hatred of me—I could see it flashing from her eyes, even as she drank in my words with the most avid attention. She insisted that I should keep on talking, that I should tell her everything, in the way of thoughts and images, that entered my mind. And I talked on, almost without thinking; or rather, it was my thought speaking in me, as from a need to relax its own convulsive tension:

"You stand at a window; you gaze upon the world; you believe that it is as it seems to you. You see people passing down there in the street,

very small in your vision which, from that high window where you are standing, is a large one. That
largeness is something that you cannot help feeling
in yourself; for if a friend should happen to pass
just now, down there in the street, and you should
recognize him, he would not seem to you, viewed
from your altitude, any larger than one of your
fingers. Ah, but if it should occur to you to call down
to him and say, 'Tell me something; how do I look
to you, standing up here at this window—?' It does
not occur to you, because you do not think of that
image which passers-by in the street have, all the
while, of that window and of you who stand there
gazing out. The thing to do is to make an effort to
detach from one's self the conditions which make
for the reality of those who pass down below, and
who live for a moment in your wide-sweeping vision
as tiny transients in a street. The reason you do not
make this effort is that you have no inkling of that
picture which they form of you and of your window,
one among so many, a small one and so very high,
and a picture of you as very, very small, standing
up there with a diminutive arm waving in the air."

She saw herself in my description, as very, very
small, at a high window, with a diminutive arm in
the air; and she laughed.

There were flashes, vibrations; and then, silence
fell once more upon the little room. Every so often,
like a shade, the aged aunt with whom Anna Rosa
lived would put in an appearance; she was fat,
apathetic, with enormous, horribly squinting eyes.
She would stand for a moment upon the threshold,

in the fluid semi-darkness, with her pale, puffy hands upon her abdomen and looking like nothing so much as a deep-sea monster in an aquarium; and then, without a word, she would go away.

With this aunt, Anna Rosa exchanged but very few words in the course of the day. She lived in herself, with herself, reading and weaving fantastic visions, but ever intolerant of the things she read as of her visions; she would go out to make a few purchases or to call upon this or that woman friend; but her friends impressed her as being silly and empty-headed, and she took a delight in shocking them; and then, she would come home, feeling tired and disgusted with everything. She had certain insuperable aversions, which would come out in the form of a burst of temper on an unforeseen veering at some allusion; it is possible that she owed these to her reading in the medical books which she had found in the library left her by her father, who had been a physician. She insisted she would never marry.

I am unable to say what sort of idea she had formed of me. She looked upon me, I am sure, with an extraordinary degree of interest, so befuddled did I impress her as being those days, in my thoughts and in my uncertainty with regard to everything. This uncertainty in me, which fled every restraint, every buttress, and which henceforth, as if by instinct, was to recede from every consistent form as the sea recedes from its banks—this uncertainty, which babbled in my eyes, undoubtedly exercised an attraction for her; but upon occasion, as I looked at her, I somehow had the strange impression that she was finding it a little amusing; for it was, after all, something to laugh at, rather, having at the foot of her bed a man in so incredible a state of mind, so wholly torn asunder, who did not know how he was going to live tomorrow, when, having by Sclepis' aid drawn his money from the bank, he should be at once despoiled and freed of everything.

For she was sure that I would go through with it to the bitter end, like the perfect madman that I was. And this amused her tremendously. Not only this; she felt a certain pride in it all for the reason that, from her talks with my wife, she had divined, if not exactly this, the fact that I was, in any event, not an ordinary sort of fellow, but one that was different from other people, to whom one might look, some day or other, for something out of the ordinary. And it was because she wished to prove to others, and especially to my wife, that she was right in her estimate of me that she had sent for me in such haste, to inform me of the plans that were being laid against me and to urge me to go to see the Monsignor. She was highly satisfied with me now, as she saw me there at the foot of her bed, steadfast and placidly waiting for what must necessarily come, without any thought for anything or anybody.

And yet, it was she, none other, who conceived the desire to kill me. It came about when, from that satisfaction which I afforded her, and which made her laugh a little, she passed on to a great commiseration for me, by way of charmed response to what she must surely have read in my eyes, as I sat there gazing at her as from an infinite distance and an ageless expanse of time.

I do not know exactly how it happened. It was when I, gazing at her from that distance, spoke to her words which I no longer remember, words in which she must have sensed a consuming passion to give the all of life within me, all that I was capable of being, in order to become one, as she might will me, and for myself truly no one at all, no one at all. I only know that from her bed she stretched forth her arms to me; I know she drew me to her.

From that bed, a moment later, I rolled back blindly, grievously wounded in the chest by a bullet from that little revolver which she kept under her pillow.

They must have been true, the reasons which she gave in her own defense, that she was impelled to slay me by a sudden, instinctive horror of an act to which she felt herself being drawn, through the strange fascination which everything that I had been telling her, those days, held for her.

BOOK EIGHTH

I

The Judge Would Like to Take His Time

THE reproach of haste is not one that is commonly made in connection with the ordinary course of justice. The judge whose duty it was to give instructions in the case against Anna Rosa, an upright man by nature and by precept, wished to be as conscientious as possible in the matter, and insisted upon squandering months and months of time, before he was ready to review the evidence, after having, of course, heard it all, including the testimony of the various witnesses.

It had not been possible, however, to get any sort of answer out of me to the first interrogatory that they had wanted to put to me, after I had been hastily removed from Anna Rosa's little room to the hospital. When the doctors finally permitted me to talk, the first answer that I gave, in place of embarrassing my questioner, embarrassed me.

This is the way it was. The transition with Anna Rosa had been so lightning-like, from that commiseration which had led her to stretch out her arms to me from her bed to that instinctive impulse which had impelled her to commit upon me that act of violence, that I, blinded by the sense of being near the warmth of her most provocative person, really had had neither the time nor the means of ascertaining how she had managed to extract the revolver from under her pillow and fire at me. And so, since it did not seem to be conceivable that, after having lured me to her, she should have wanted to kill me, it was with the most straightforward sincerity that I gave my questioner the explanation of the affair which appeared most likely, namely, that my wound, like the one in her foot, had been accidental, owing to the admittedly reprehensible fact that she was in the habit of keeping that revolver under her pillow; and that it surely must have been I who, in an effort to lift up the bedridden woman, who had asked me to come and sit on the side of her bed, had bumped against the weapon and caused it to go off.

For me, the lie (a dutiful lie) lay only in the last part of my answer; to my questioner, however, it appeared to have been so brazenly manufactured out of whole cloth that I was given a severe reprimand. He let me understand that, as it happened, the court was in possession of an explicit confession from the accused. And I thereupon, due to an irresistible need of establishing my sincerity, was so artless in my astonishment as to manifest the liveliest curiosity concerning the reasons which the accused might have given for her violent attack upon me.

The answer to this question was a loud snort, which all but gave me a face-bath.

"Hah, so you merely wanted to set her up on the bed?"

I was overcome.

The court, it devolved, was similarly in possession of an initial deposition made by my wife, who now, if never before, with factual proof at hand, could surely testify in all good conscience to the fact that my infatuation for Anna Rosa was of long standing. As a result of it all, the court undoubtedly would have remained convinced that Anna Rosa had attempted to slay me in self-defense, when brutally attacked by me, had not Anna Rosa herself assured the judge upon her oath that there really had been no such attack, but that the whole thing had been due to the remarkable fascination which my extremely curious views of life had exercised upon her, a fascination to which she had so far yielded as to be led to commit that act of madness.

The conscientious judge, not satisfied with the summary account which Anna Rosa had been able to give him of those views of mine, had deemed it his duty to seek more accurate and first-hand information, and had wanted to come and talk to me in person.

II

The Green Woolen Coverlet

I HAD been taken home from the hospital on a litter;
but now I had already entered upon my con-
valescence, had left my bed, and at this time was
blissfully reposing in an easy chair near the window,
with a green woolen coverlet over my legs.

I was like a drunken man, frolicking in a sweet
and tranquil, dreamlike void. Spring had come
back, and the sun's first warming rays brought me
an indescribably delightful languor. I was almost
afraid of being struck by the fresh, mild, limpid air
that came in through the half-closed window, and
kept myself sheltered against it; but from time to
time, I would raise my eyes to survey the vivid blue
of the March sky, traversed by graceful, light-
flecked clouds. Then, I would look at my hands,
which were still bloodless and shaking; I would drop
them upon my thighs, and with the end of my finger
would lightly caress the green down of that woolen
coverlet. I had a glimpse of the countryside, seemingly one boundless expanse of grain; and fondling
it with my eyes, I reveled in it all, really feeling
as if I were in the midst of all that grain, with a
sense of timeless distance that filled me with the
gentlest sort of anguish.

Ah, to lose one's self there, to stretch out and
abandon one's self, there in the grass, under the

silent heavens, to fill one's soul with all that reach of blue, letting every thought, every memory go shipwreck!

I ask you now, could that judge have happened in at a more inopportune time? I am sorry, as I think back on it, if he went away from my house that day with the impression that I had wanted to make sport of him.

He was like a mole, with those two tiny hands of his which were always up near his mouth, and his little, leaden, almost sightless, half-shut eyes. The whole of his meager, little, ill-clad figure was deformed, one shoulder being higher than the other. In the street, he sidled in his walk, as dogs do, although everybody said that, morally, no one could walk a straighter line than he.

My views of life?

"Ah, your Honor," I said, "believe me, it is not possible for me to repeat them now. Look here! Look here!"

And I showed him the green woolen coverlet, running my hand over it, delicately.

"It is your duty, is it, to gather and arrange those details of which the court tomorrow will make use in giving its decision? And you have come to ask me for my views of life, those views which to the accused were sufficient reason for killing me? But if I were to repeat them now, your Honor, I am very much afraid that, instead of killing me, you would kill yourself, out of remorse from having for so many years held that office of yours. No, no, I shall not tell you what they are, your Honor! It is a good thing that you wear cotton in your ears, so that you may not have to hear the terrible breaking of a certain surf at the foot of the dikes, beyond those watermarks which you, like the good judge you are, have staked out and set up for the guidance of your most scrupulous conscience. They may come caving in—did you know that?—at a moment when the tempest rages, as it did with Signorina Anna Rosa. What surf? Ah, that of the great waters, your Honor! You have canalized them well, in your emotions, in the obligations which you have laid upon yourself, in the habits which you have marked out for yourself; but there comes the moment of full tide, your Honor, when the waters overflow the bank, overflow the bank and overturn everything. I am the one that knows. Everything is submerged for me, your Honor! I have cast myself into those waters, and now, I am swimming in them, swimming in them. And if you only knew how very far away I am already! I can scarcely see you any longer. Farewell, your Honor, farewell!"

He sat there stupefied, staring at me as one stares at an incurable. Hoping to break the painful tension for him, I smiled; with both my hands, I lifted up the coverlet from my knees and showed it to him again.

"I beg your pardon," I said, "but really—just see how green this woolen coverlet is! Don't you think it's pretty?"

III

Abnegation

I CONSOLED myself with the reflection that all this should facilitate Anna Rosa's acquittal. But on the other hand, there was Sclepis, who a number of times, with his gristly frame all a-tremble, had come running to inform me that I had rendered and was continuing to render more difficult than ever for him the task of my salvation. Could it be possible I was not aware of the enormous scandal which had been provoked by that misadventure of mine, and this at the very moment when I should have been giving proof of the fact that I had a better head on my shoulders than any of them? What had I done, on the contrary, but prove that my wife was right in going home to her father, after my disgraceful conduct toward her? I had betrayed her; and it had been solely to cut a figure in the eyes of that giddy-headed girl that I had insisted I did not want to be called a usurer any more! And it was thanks to my blind and guilty passion that I was stubbornly bent upon ruining myself and others, notwithstanding the fact that this same guilty passion had come near costing me my life!

And now, accordingly, as Sclepis saw it, with the lot of them pitted against him as they were, there was nothing left to do except to acknowledge my deplorable faults; he saw no other salvation, no other escape for me than to make a free and open confession of my sins. But it was necessary, if this confession were not to prove dangerous, that I at the same time should give evidence of a vital and urgent soul-need, the need of an heroic atonement, in order to give him the strength of mind to ask of the others the sacrifice of their own interests.

I did nothing but nod my head affirmatively to all he said to me, without troubling to observe the precise point at which what had been at the start a purely dialectical argumentation had gradually, as he warmed up to his subject, become in him a really sincere conviction. I only know that he appeared ever more satisfied, even if there was, possibly, a certain inner perplexity as to whether this satisfaction of his were due to an actual charitable feeling or to pride in his own intellectual sagacity.

The decision reached was that I should set an example, and the most impressive kind of example, of penitence and self-abnegation, by making a donation of everything, including my house and all my other property, for the founding, with what I should have from the liquidation of the bank, of a paupers' retreat, with a public kitchen open all the year round, not only for the benefit of the inmates, but for all the poor who might have need of it; and there should be a vestiary as well, for both sexes and all ages, to accommodate so many a year; and I myself should take a room there, sleeping without distinction, like any other beggar, upon a cot, eating my soup like the others from a wooden bowl, and putting on the communal habit designed for one of my age and sex.

What annoyed me more than anything else was that this total abnegation of mine was interpreted as being a true penitence; whereas, if I gave all and opposed nothing, it was because I was by now as far removed as could be from anything that might have a meaning or a value for others; I not only was absolutely alienated from myself and from everything, but I had a horror of remaining in any manner *someone,* in possession of something.

No longer willing anything, I no longer felt able to speak. And so, I kept silent, as I admiringly surveyed that diaphanous old prelate, who possessed so great a power of will and the power to exert that will so artfully and so subtly, and this not for his own private advantage, nor perhaps so much by way of doing good to others, but rather, for the sake of the merit from it all which would accrue to that house of God of which he was a most faithful and a most zealous servant.

Behold him, then: for himself, no one.

Could it be that this was the path that led to becoming one for all?

But there was in this priest too much pride of his own power and his own wisdom. While living for others, he still wanted to be one to himself, to be clearly distinguished from others by his wisdom and his power, not to mention that more than proved fidelity of his and his greater zeal for the cause.

Which was the reason why I continued, as I did, to look upon him with a mingled pain and admiration.

IV

No Conclusion

ANNA ROSA, of course, was acquitted; but I cannot help feeling that her acquittal was partly due to the hilarity that prevailed in the courtroom, when, summoned to give my testimony, I made my appearance in the institutional vizored cap, wooden sandals and sky-blue blouse. I have not since that day glanced in a mirror, and the desire to know what has become of my face and the whole appearance that once was mine does not so much as enter my head. My appearance to others must have been greatly changed, and in a way comically enough, to judge from the astonishment and the bursts of laughter with which I was greeted. Nevertheless, they all insisted upon calling me Moscarda still, although the name Moscarda surely held for everyone a different signification than before; and it seems to me they might have spared that poor nobody of a pauper, as he stood there smilingly in his wooden sandals and his sky-blue blouse, the pain of having to turn around once again at the sound of that name, as if it really belonged to him.

No name. No memory today of yesterday's name; of today's name tomorrow. If the name is the thing, if a name in us is the concept of everything that is situated without us, if without a name there is no concept, and the thing remains blindly indistinct and undefined within us, very well, then, let men take that name which I once bore and engrave it as an epitaph on the brow of that pictured me that they beheld; let them leave it there in peace, and let them not speak of it again. For a name is no more than that, an epitaph. Something befitting the dead. One who has reached a conclusion. I am alive, and I reach no conclusion. Life knows no conclusion. Nor does it know anything of names. This tree, tremulous breathing of new leaves. I am this tree. Tree, cloud; tomorrow, book or breeze; the book I read, the breeze I drink in. Living wholly without, a vagabond.

The Shelter stands in the open country, in a very pleasant place. I come out every morning at daybreak, for the reason that I wish thus to preserve my soul, with all the freshness of half-seen things at dawn, still held in the night's grasp, before the dazzling sun has come to dry their humid breath. Those water-laden clouds, resting like a leaden weight upon the livid heights, casting into wider and brighter relief that verdant tract of sky, amid the lingering shadows of the night. And these grass blades here, delicately dripping with moisture, they too; breathing freshness of watersides. And that stolid-eyed donkey, which has remained standing there quietly all night, and which now lets out a bray in this silence, which is so very, very near, a silence that little by little, but without surprise, appears to be going away and lifting, at the coming of the light which barely floods the deserted and wonder-wrapped countryside. And these wagon-paths here, between the dark hedges and the heaps of sundered stone, which appear to be standing still, not going, in their own deep-gutted tracks. And the air is fresh. And all, from second to second, is as it is, revived to take on appearance. I quickly turn my eyes in order not to see again anything coming to an apparitional halt and dying. So only can I go on living, henceforward. By being reborn second by second. By seeing to it that thought does not once more start working in me, and within me refashion the void that goes with the vanity of building things.

The city is far away. There comes to me occasionally, upon the vesper calm, the sound of its bells. I, however, no longer hear those bells within me, but without, ringing for themselves and perhaps trembling with joy in their resounding cavities, in a beautiful blue sky filled with a warm sun, to the twittering of swallows or swaying heavily to wind and cloud, so high, so high, in their aerial belfries. To think of death, to pray. It may be that there is one who yet has need of this, and it is to his need that the bells give voice. I no longer have any such need, for the reason that I am dying every instant, and being born anew and without memories: alive and whole, no longer in myself, but in everything outside.

The End.

CPSIA information can be obtained
at www.ICGtesting.com
Printed in the USA
BVHW05s0240300718
523009BV00015B/156/P

9 781162 784854